USDA

United States
Department of
Agriculture

Forest Service

Northern
Research Station

Resource Bulletin NRS-49

Missouri's Forest 1999-2003

Part B

Andrew D. Hill

Mark H. Hansen

W. Keith Moser

Gary Brand

Ronald E. McRoberts

Abstract

This report presents the methods used in the 1999-2003 inventory of the forest resources of Missouri along with tables of important forest attribute estimates and discussion of quality of these estimates. This inventory is part of the Forest Inventory and Analysis (FIA) program conducted by U.S. Forest Service, a national program to continuously inventory and report on all forest land in the nation. Additional information from this inventory and other FIA inventories conducted by can be found at http://fia.fs.fed.us/.

The Authors

ANDREW D. HILL, research scientist, MARK D. HANSEN, research forester, retired, W. KEITH MOSER, research forester, KEITH BRAND, research forester, and RONALD E. McROBERTS, mathematical statistician, are with the U.S. Forest Service Northern Research Station's Forest Inventory and Analysis unit in St. Paul, MN. For more information on this report, contact Andrew Hill at adhill@fs.fed.us.

CONTENTS

Forest Inventory Methods...1

    Strategic Model...1

    Plot Configuration 2

    Sample Design..2

    Three-Phase Inventory 3

    Estimation 5

    Integration with Previous Inventories 6

Quality of the Estimates...8

    Sampling Error..8

    Measurement Error...9

    Prediction Error 11

    Nonresponse Error..11

Glossary 13

Literature Cited...22

Tables 24

FOREST INVENTORY METHODS
Strategic Model

The Forest Inventory and Analysis program of the Northern Research Station (NRS-FIA) is part of the national enhanced FIA program that focuses on a set of six strategic objectives (McRoberts 2005):

1. A standard set of variables with nationally consistent meanings and measurements
2. Field inventories of all forested lands
3. Nationally consistent estimation
4. Adherence to national precision standards
5. Consistent reporting and data distribution
6. Credibility with users and stakeholders

To ensure that these objectives are achieved, 10 strategic approaches have been prescribed:

1. A national set of prescribed core variables with a national field manual that prescribes measurement procedures and protocols for each variable
2. National plot configuration
3. Nationally consistent sampling design
4. Estimation using standardized formulae for sample-based estimators
5. A national database of FIA data with core standards and user-friendly public access
6. A national information management system
7. A nationally consistent set of tables of estimates of prescribed core variables
8. Publication of statewide tables of estimates of prescribed core variables at 5-year
9. Documentation of the technical aspects of the FIA program including procedures, protocols, and techniques
10. Peer review and publication of the technical documentation for general access

The result of the strategic objectives and approaches is an inventory program with identifiably new features and a nationally consistent plot configuration, a nationally consistent sampling design for all lands, annual measurement of a proportion of plots in each state, nationally consistent estimation techniques and algorithms, and integration of the ground sampling components of the FIA inventory and detection monitoring by the USDA Forest Service's Forest Health Monitoring (FHM) program.

Plot Configuration

The national FIA plot design (Fig. 1) consists of four 24-ft-radius subplots configured as a central subplot and three peripheral subplots. Centers of the peripheral subplots are located at distances of 120 ft and at azimuths of 0, 120, and 240 from the center of the central subplot. Each tree with diameter at breast height (d.b.h.) 5 inches or greater is measured on these subplots. Each subplot contains a 6.8-ft-radius microplot with center located 12 ft east of the subplot center on which each tree with d.b.h. between 1 and 5 inches is measured. Factors that differentiate forest conditions include forest type, stand-size class, stand origin, land use, ownership, and density. Forest conditions that occur on any of the four subplots are identified and recorded; if the area of the condition is 1 acre or greater, the condition is mapped on the subplot.

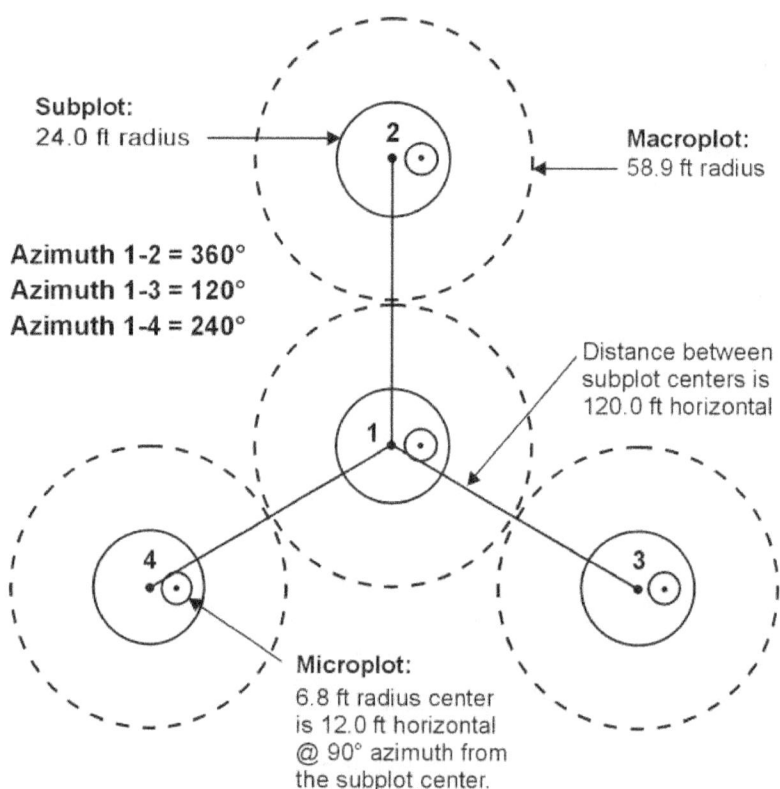

Subplot:
24.0 ft radius

Macroplot:
58.9 ft radius

Azimuth 1-2 = 360°
Azimuth 1-3 = 120°
Azimuth 1-4 = 240°

Distance between subplot centers is 120.0 ft horizontal

Microplot:
6.8 ft radius center is 12.0 ft horizontal @ 90° azimuth from the subplot center.

Figure 1.—National FIA plot design (adapted from Bechtold and Patterson 2005).

Sample Design

Historic sampling errors indicate that a sampling intensity of about one plot per 6,000 acres is required to satisfy national FIA precision guidelines. Therefore, FIA divided the area of the United States into nonoverlapping, 5,937-acre hexagons and established a plot in each hexagon as follows: 1) if an existing FHM plot was located in a hexagon, it was selected; 2) if there was no FHM plot in the hexagon, the existing FIA plot from the previous periodic inventory nearest the hexagon center was selected; and 3) if neither an FHM nor an FIA plot was located in the hexagon, a new FIA plot was established at a random location in the hexagon (Brand et al. 2000, McRoberts 1999). This array of field plots is designated the federal base sample and is considered an equal probability sample; its measurement is funded by the federal government.

The Federal base sample was divided into five interpenetrating, nonoverlapping panels or subsamples, each of which provides complete, systematic coverage of a state. Each year, plots in a single panel are measured and panels are selected on a 5-year, rotating basis (McRoberts 1999). For estimation purposes, the measurement of each panel of plots is considered an independent, equal probability sample of all lands in a state.

Three-Phase Inventory

FIA conducts inventories in three phases. Phase 1 uses remotely sensed data to obtain initial plot land-cover observations and to stratify land area in the population of interest to increase the precision of estimates. In Phase 2, field crews visit the physical locations of permanent field plots to measure traditional inventory variables such as tree species, diameter, and height. In Phase 3, field crews visit a subset of Phase 2 plots to obtain measurements for an additional suite of variables associated with forest and ecosystem health. The three phases of the enhanced FIA program as implemented in this inventory are discussed in greater detail in the sections that follow.

Phase 1

Aerial photographs, digital orthoquads (DOQs: digitally scanned aerial photographs) and satellite imagery are used for initial plot measurement via remotely sensed data and stratification. Phase 1 plot measurement consists of observations of conditions at the plot locations using aerial photographs or DOQs. Analysts determine a digitized geographic location for each field plot and a human interpreter assigns the plot a land cover/use. All plot locations that could possibly contain accessible forest land are selected for further measurement via field-crew visits in Phase 2. Lands satisfying FIA's definition of forest land use include commercial timberland, some pastured land with trees, forest plantations, unproductive forested land, and reserved, noncommercial forested land. In addition, forest land use requires minimum stocking levels, a 1-acre minimum area, and a minimum bole-to-bole width of 120 ft with continuous canopy. Forest land excludes wooded strips and windbreaks less than 120 ft wide and idle farmland or other previously nonforest land that currently is below minimum stocking levels.

The combination of natural variability among plots and budgetary constraints prohibits measurement of a sufficient number of plots to satisfy national precision standards for most inventory variables unless the estimation process is enhanced using ancillary data. Thus, the land area is stratified by using remotely sensed data to facilitate stratified estimation. Because FIA uses a quasi-systematic sampling design, stratified random sampling is not an option. Nevertheless, even with systematic sampling, stratified estimation may increase precision.

A stratification scheme based on satellite imagery is used in the estimation as proposed by Hansen and Wendt (2000) and is applied to the National Land Cover Data (NLCD) as suggested by McRoberts et al. (2002). The NLCD is a digital land-cover map of the

3

conterminous United States in which 30- by 30-m pixels are assigned to 21 land-cover classes. The land-cover classification was produced by the U.S. Geological Survey and was based on nominal 1992 Landsat 5 Thematic Mapper (TM) satellite imagery and a variety of ancillary data (Vogelmann et al. 2001). Four strata are created using a three-step process: 1) aggregate NLCD classes with trees into a forest stratum, and the remaining classes into a nonforest stratum; 2) reclassify isolated groups of three or fewer pixels into their surrounding forest or nonforest class to comply with the FIA criterion that forest land must be at least 1 acre; and 3) create a forest-edge stratum by removing from the forest stratum a 2-pixel-wide band on the forest side of the forest/nonforest boundary and create a nonforest-edge stratum by removing from the nonforest stratum a 2-pixel-wide band on the nonforest side of the forest/nonforest boundary.

In addition to classifying every pixel into one of the four strata, FIA assigns every pixel to an ownership strata based on the Protected Areas Database (PAD) described by DellaSala et al. 2001. In Missouri, the PAD was used to classify pixels into three ownership classes: 1) U.S. Forest Service (1,318,000 acres); 2) other public owners (1,441,000 acres); and 3) private owners (41,783,000 acres). Every pixel also was assigned to a county based on the location of the pixel center.

Stratified estimation requires that two tasks be accomplished: each plot must be assigned to a single stratum, and the proportion of the estimation unit in each stratum must be calculated. The first task is accomplished by assigning each plot to the stratum assigned for the pixel containing the center of the center subplot. The second task is accomplished by calculating the proportion of pixels in each stratum. The population total estimate for a variable is calculated as the sum across all strata of the product of each stratum's observed proportion (from Phase 1) and the variable's estimated mean per unit area for the stratum (from Phase 2).

Phase 2

In Phase 2, field crews record a variety of data for plot locations determined in Phase 1 to include accessible forest land use. Before visiting plot locations, field crews consult county land records to determine the ownership of plots and then seek permission from landowners to measure plots on their lands. Field crews determine the location of the geographic center of the center subplot using geographic positioning system (GPS) receivers. They record condition-level observations that include land cover, forest type, stand origin, stand age, stand-size class, site productivity class, history of forest disturbance, and ground land use for every condition (major land use or forest stand at least 1 acre in size) that occurs on the plot. They also record information on condition boundary on plots with multiple conditions. For each tree, field crews record a variety of observations and measurements, including condition, species, live/dead status, lean, diameter, height, crown ratio (percent of tree height represented by crown), crown class (dominant, codominant, suppressed), damage, and decay status. Office staff use statistical models based on field-crew measurements to calculate values for additional variables, including individual-tree volume, estimates per unit area of the number of trees, volume, and biomass by plot, condition, species group, and live/dead status. Additional information on the collection procedures used in Phase 2 of this inventory is available at http://www.nrs.fs.fed.us/fia/data-collection.

Phase 3

The third phase of the enhanced FIA program focuses on forest health. Phase 3 is administered cooperatively by FIA, other Forest Service programs, other Federal agencies, state natural resource agencies, and universities, and is partially integrated with the FHM program. The latter consists of four interrelated and complementary activities: detection, evaluation, intensive site monitoring, and research on monitoring techniques. Detection monitoring consists of systematic aerial and ground surveys designed to collect baseline information on the current condition of forest ecosystems and to detect changes from those baselines over time. Evaluation monitoring studies examine the extent, severity, and probable causes of changes in forest health identified through the detection monitoring surveys. Intensive site monitoring studies regionally specific ecological processes at a network of sites located in representative forested ecosystems. Research on monitoring techniques focuses on developing and refining indicator measurements to improve the efficiency and reliability of data collection and analysis at all levels of the program.

The ground-survey portion of the detection monitoring program was integrated into the FIA program as Phase 3 in 1999. The Phase 3 sample consists of a 1:16 subset of the Phase 2 plots with one Phase 3 plot for about every 95,000 acres. Phase 3 measurements are obtained by field crews during the growing season and include an extended suite of ecological data: lichen diversity and abundance, soil quality (erosion, compaction, and chemistry), vegetation diversity and structure, and down woody material. The incidence and severity of ozone injury for selected bioindicator species also are monitored as part of an associated sampling scheme. Because each Phase 3 plot also is a Phase 2 plot, the entire suite of Phase 2 measurements is collected on each Phase 3 plot at the same time as the Phase 3 measurements. Additional information on the collection procedures used in Phase 3 of this inventory are available at http:// www.nrs.fs.fed.us/fia/data-collection.

The Phase 3 suite of variables address specific criteria outlined by the Montreal Process Working Group for the conservation and sustainable management of temperate and boreal forests, and is based on the concept of indicator variables. Observations of an indicator variable represent an index of ecosystem functions that can be monitored over time to assess trends. Indicator variables are used in conjunction with each other, Phase 2 data, data from FHM evaluation monitoring studies, and ancillary data to address ecological issues such as vegetation diversity, fuel loading, regional air-quality gradients, and carbon storage. The Phase 2 and Phase 3 data of the enhanced FIA program serve as the Nation's environmental report card and are a primary source of reporting data for Montreal Process criteria.

Estimation

The majority of the estimates and analysis of forest recourses presented in this report, including all of the estimates in Tables 1 through 61 are based on data observed from October 1, 1998 to September 30, 2003 on the 9,486 Phase 2 plots (Fig. 2) across Missouri. In fiscal year 1999 (October 1, 1998 to September 30, 1999) about 1,500 plots were observed. In each of the next four fiscal years (2000 to 2003), additional support from the Missouri Department of Conservation doubled the intensity in the southeastern portion of the State; about 2,000 plots were observed in each of those years. The analysis of forest

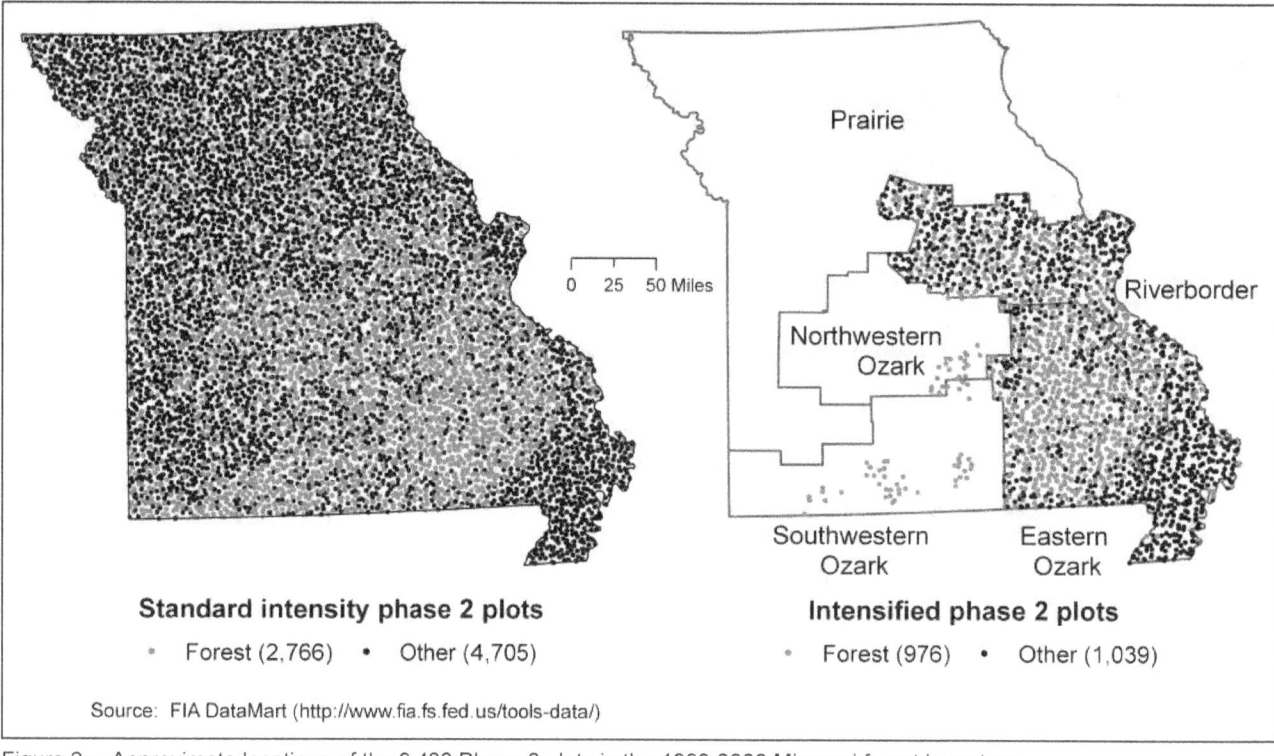

Figure 2.—Approximate locations of the 9,486 Phase 2 plots in the 1999-2003 Missouri forest inventory.

health issues that relate to down wood materials, soils, ozone damage, and crown condition are based on data observed on the 371 Phase 3 plots (Fig. 3) that are a subsample of the Phase 2 plots.

The Phase 2 observations are distributed evenly across the 5-year period when plots were measured. These plots are located within 267 estimation strata (Table A) defined by combinations of the four Phase 1 classes (nonforest, nonforest edge, forest edge, and forest), a land-ownership classification created from the PAD, and county groups. Procedures described in Bechtold and Patterson (2005) for stratified estimation with observed stratum areas were used in conjunction with the strata in Table A to produce all estimates. Table A shows the total area and number of plots within each strata.

Integration with Previous Inventories

In 2003, NRS-FIA completed measurement of the fifth panel of inventory plots in Missouri. The 2003 panel, along with those surveyed in 1999, 2000, 2001, and 2002, completed data collection for the fifth inventory of Missouri's forests. Previous inventories of Missouri's forest resources were completed in 1947, 1959, 1972, and 1989 (USDA For. Serv. 1948, Gansner 1965, Spencer and Essex 1976, Spencer et al. 1992). Data from new inventories often are compared with data from earlier inventories to determine trends in forest resources. However, for the comparisons to be valid, the procedures used in the two inventories must be similar. As a result of our ongoing efforts to improve the efficiency and reliability of the inventory, several changes in procedures and definitions have been made since the Missouri inventory in 1989 (Spencer et al. 1992). Although these changes will have little impact on

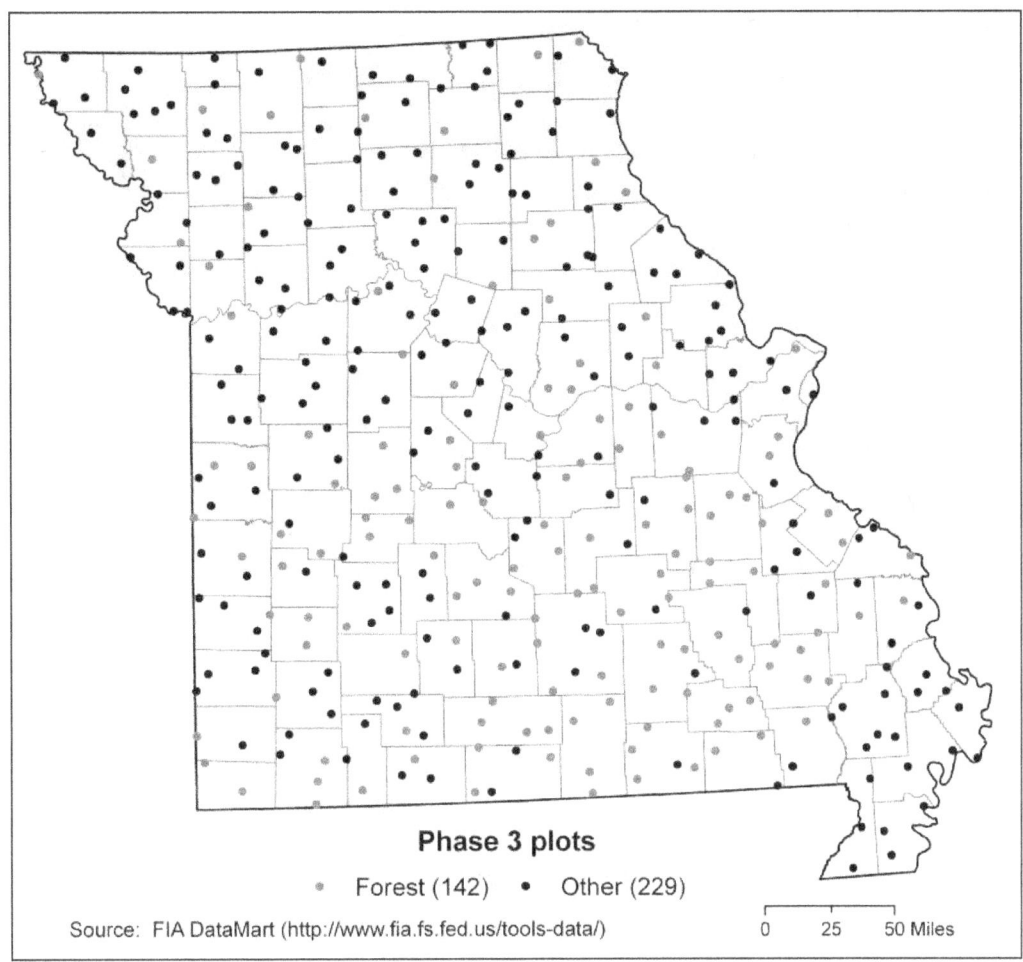

Phase 3 plots

● Forest (142)   ● Other (229)

Source: FIA DataMart (http://www.fia.fs.fed.us/tools-data/)

0   25   50 Miles

Figure 3.—Approximate locations of the 371 phase 3 plots in the 1999-2003 Missouri forest inventory.

statewide estimates of forest area, timber volume, and tree biomass, they may significantly impact plot classification variables such as forest type and stand-size class. For estimating growth, removals, and mortality, the 1989 inventory (Spencer et al. 1992) was processed using estimation/summary routines for the 1999-2003 inventory. Although these changes allow limited comparison of inventory estimates among separate inventories in this report, it is inappropriate to directly compare all portions of the 1999-2003 data with those published for earlier inventories.

For addional information on the sample protocols and estimation procedures for the first two phases of the FIA program, see Bechtold and Patterson (2005). For additional information on Phase 3 indicator sampling protocols, see USDA For. Serv. (2005) and Woodall and Williams (2005).

QUALITY OF THE ESTIMATES

The quality of this report's estimates is addressed by quantifying associated errors. Two general types of error, random variability (precision) and estimation bias (accuracy), should be of general concern to all users of any estimates. Random variability refers to the general imprecision of the estimate, which would occur if the entire sampling and estimation process were to be repeated many times. Estimation bias refers to the difference between the estimate and the "true value" in the absence of this random variability and refers to the overestimation or underestimation inherent in the entire estimation process.

Errors in the estimates presented in this report (both estimation bias and random variability) are affected by various sources. The four primary sources of error common to all sample-based estimates are sampling, measurement, prediction, and nonresponse error. A section is devoted to each of these sources of error. Included in each section is a definition of the source of error in the context of the FIA inventory as well as a discussion of methods used to quantify and/or reduce that source of error. Measures of sampling, measurement, and prediction errors associated with various attributes are presented and issues of possible bias related to nonresponse are addressed.

Sampling Error

The process of sampling (selecting a random subset of a population and calculating estimates from this subset) causes estimates to contain error they would not have if every member of the population had been observed and included in the estimate. The 1999-2003 FIA inventory of Missouri is based on a sample of 9,486 plots located randomly across the State (a total area of 44.6 million acres), or a sampling rate of about one plot for every 4,700 acres.

The procedures for statistical estimation outlined in the previous section and described in detail in Bechtold and Patterson (2005) provide the estimates of the population totals and means presented in this report. Along with every estimate is an associated sampling error that is typically expressed as a percentage of the estimated value but that can also be expressed in the same units as the estimate or as a confidence interval (the estimated value plus or minus the sampling error). This sampling error is the primary measure of the reliability of an estimate. A sampling error can be interpreted to mean that the chances are two in three that had a 100-percent inventory been taken using these methods, the results would have been within the limits indicated.

The sampling errors for State-level estimates of the major attributes presented in this report are presented in Table B. Table 65 presents sampling errors for these estimates at the forest survey unit and county group level.

Estimates for classifications smaller than the State totals in Table B will have larger sampling errors. For example, Table 65 shows the sampling error for timberland area in any county is higher than that for total timberland area in the State. To compute an approximate sampling error for an estimate that is smaller than a State total, use the following formula:

$$E = \frac{(SE)\sqrt{(\text{State total estimate})}}{\sqrt{(\text{Smaller estimate})}} \qquad (1)$$

where:

E = approximate sampling error for smaller estimate

SE = sampling error for State total estimate

For example, to compute the error on the area of forest land in the oak hickory forest-type group for the State, proceed as follows:

The total area of the oak-hickory forest-type group in the State from Table 3 is 11,469,300 acres. The total area of all forest land in the state from Table 3 is 14,576,500 acres. The State total error for forest land area from Table B is 0.80 percent.

Using formula (1):

$$\text{Sampling error} = E = \frac{(0.80)\sqrt{(14,576,500)}}{\sqrt{(11,469,300)}} = 0.90 \text{ percent.}$$

The estimators used by FIA are unbiased under the assumptions that the sample plots are a random sample of the total population and the observed value for any plot is the true value for that plot. Deviations from these basic assumptions are not reflected in the computation of sampling errors. The following sections on measurement, prediction, and nonresponse error address possible departures from these basic assumptions.

Measurement Error

Errors associated with the methods and instruments used to observe and record the sample attributes are called measurement errors. On FIA plots, attributes such as the diameter and height of a tree are measured with different instruments, and other attributes such as species and crown class are observed without the aid of an instrument. On a typical FIA plot, 30 to 70 trees are observed with 15 to 20 attributes recorded on each tree. Also, many attributes that describe the plot and conditions on the plot are observed. Errors in any of these observations affect the quality of the estimates. If a measurement is biased (such as tree diameter consistently taken at an incorrect place on the tree), the estimates that use this observation (such as volume) will reflect this bias. Even if measurements are unbiased, high levels of random error in the measurements will add to the total random error of the estimation process.

To ensure that all FIA observations are made to the highest standards possible, a regular program of quality control and quality assurance is an integral part of all FIA data-collection efforts. This program begins with the documentation of protocols and procedures used in the inventory followed by extensive crew training. To assess the quality of the data collected by these trained crews, a random sample of at least 4 percent of all plots is measured independently by a different qualified crew. These independent measurements are referred to as blind checks; the purpose of which is to assess the quality of field measurements. The second measurement on blind check plots is made by a "QA crew." In all cases, QA crews have as much or more experience and training in FIA field measurements as that of standard FIA crews.

The quality of field measurements is assessed nationally through a set of measurement quality objectives (MQOs) that are set for every data item we collect. Each MQO consists of two parts: a tolerance or acceptable level of measurement error and an objective in terms of the percent of measurements within tolerance. Blind check measurements are used to observe how often individual field crews are meeting these objectives and to assess the overall compliance among all crews. Table C shows the compliance rates for various measurements used to compute the estimates included in this report and in other NRS-FIA reports. The columns labeled "Missouri" are based on blind check measurements of plots used in this report. The columns labeled "All Midwestern States" are based on all measurements by FIA crews within the entire 11-state area surrounding Missouri (North Dakota, South Dakota, Nebraska, Kansas, Minnesota, Iowa, Missouri, Wisconsin, Illinois, Michigan, and Indiana) where the Northern Research Station implemented the FIA program over 1999-2003. Training and supervision of crews is a regional effort and crews often work in more than one state. Regional data quality observations reflect the overall measurement quality of all data collected by FIA in this midwestern region.

In addition to percent compliance to MQO tolerances, the blind check observations were used to test for relative bias in the field-crew measurements. Relative bias is defined here as a tendency for standard field-crew measurements to be higher or lower than measurements taken by the QA crews. The estimated relative bias and limits of 95-percent confidence intervals (based on parametric bootstrap estimates) for the relative bias are presented in Table D.

Blind check measurements do not provide direct observations of true bias in field measurements (average difference between field measurements and true values) because they are paired observations of two field measurements. The QA crew in these blind checks typically has more training and experience with FIA field measurements than the first crew, but both crews use the same methods and instruments to obtain measurements. These methods have been selected to be the best available and for use nationwide by FIA; they are commonly used by similar natural-resource inventories. A basic assumption is that when applied correctly, these methods provide unbiased observations of the attribute they are designed to measure. Under this assumption, relative bias observations in Table D provide observations of bias due to the difference in experience and training between the field and QA crews. In most cases, there is no significant bias.

Prediction Error

Errors associated with mathematical models (such as volume models) aimed at providing observations of the attributes of interest based on sample attributes are called prediction errors. Area, number of trees, volume, biomass, growth, removals, and mortality are the primary attributes of interest presented in this report. Estimates of area and number of trees are based on direct observation and do not rely on prediction models. However, FIA estimates of volume, biomass, growth, removals, and mortality use model-based predictions in the estimation process. Models are used to predict volume and biomass estimates of individual tree volumes. Change estimates such as growth, mortality, and removals are based on these model-based predictions of volume from both the current plot measurements and the measurements taken in the previous inventory.

Estimates of prediction errors associated with the volume models in this report were presented by Hahn and Hansen (1991) along with model forms, methods used in model development, and model-parameter estimates. The estimated prediction errors are based on observations of 10,453 trees measured in the 1989 Missouri statewide inventory. For gross cubic-foot volume in live trees, there was an overall overprediction of 2.5 percent across all species, with an underprediction of 4.3 percent in trees less than 10 inches in d.b.h., and an overprediction of 7.1 percent in trees 20 inches and larger in d.b.h. Similar prediction errors were observed in the board-foot estimates.

Users of FIA estimates should be aware of the possible prediction errors in those estimates. In comparing FIA estimates to other data sources, users need to be aware of the prediction models used in both estimates. If both estimates are based on the same prediction models with matching fitted parameter values, the prediction bias of one estimate should cancel out that of the other estimate. If the estimates are based on different prediction models, users should be aware of the prediction error of both models.

Nonresponse Error

Nonresponse error refers to the error caused when it is not possible to observe certain elements in the sample. In FIA, nonresponse occurs when crews are unable to measure a plot (or a portion of a plot) at a selected location. Nonresponse falls into the following three classes:

- Denied access—Entire plots or portions of plots where the field crew is unable to obtain permission from the landowner to measure trees on the plot
- Hazardous/inaccessible—Entire plots or portions of plots where conditions prevent a crew from safely accessing the plot or measuring trees on the plot
- Other—Plots where the field crew is unable to obtain a valid measurement for reasons other than those stated above

Nonresponse has two effects on the sample. First, it reduces the sample size thus increasing the sampling errors of the estimates. Second, nonresponse can bias the estimates if the portion of the population not being sampled differs from the portion being sampled.

In FIA, unlike many survey samples, nonresponse rates are relatively low. In the 1999-2003 Missouri inventory, 9,486 sample plots were selected for observation. More than 96 percent of these sample plots are included in the sample used to estimate current resources. On 339 plots, crews were unable to obtain owner permission to measure the plot or part of the plot; hazardous conditions on 14 plots prevented the crew from measuring all or part of the plot, and 2 plots were lost from the sample for other reasons.

Even an overall nonresponse rate of 1 percent can cause considerable bias if not properly accounted for. The major source of nonresponse is denied access to plots, which occurs primarily on lands in private ownership. Also, observations for plots on nonforest and water land classes rarely require crews to physically enter the land, nor is permission needed because the observation can be obtained from aerial photos or other sources of remotely sensed information.

The stratified estimation process used by FIA with strata defined by three ownership classes (National Forest, Other Public, and Private) and four Landsat TM forest cover classes (Nonforest, Nonforest Edge, Forest Edge, and Forest) reduces the possible effects of bias caused by nonresponse. Under the stratified estimation process used by FIA, nonresponses are removed from the sample, and stratum estimates (means, totals, and sampling errors) are obtained only from plots with valid observations. The net effect in the estimates of means and totals is that the average of the observed plots within the stratum (ownership-forest-cover class) becomes the estimate for all nonresponses within that stratum. The nonresponse rate in one stratum does not affect the estimate in other strata. The response rate within each stratum is presented in Table E for the Missouri 1999-2003 inventory and for all FIA inventories conducted by the Northern Research Station over the same period.

In Table 1 of this report we acknowledge denied access and hazardous as two land classes in Missouri within which we are unable to provide estimates of conditions, e.g., forest area and timber volume. However, we do report the total estimated area in each of these classes. In all other tables in the report, we do not acknowledge either of these classes, and in the estimation process we treat the sample where we do have observations as a random sample of the entire State.

The nonresponse plots in this inventory were not permanently removed from the FIA system of plots. In future inventories we will again attempt to measure these plots. At that time we may be able to obtain permission to access these plots, hazardous conditions may have changed, and other circumstances that caused us to drop plots from a specific inventory cycle may well be different.

GLOSSARY

Average annual mortality of growing stock: The average cubic-foot volume of sound wood in growing-stock trees that died in one year, between 1999 and 2003.

Average annual mortality of sawtimber: The average board-foot volume of sound wood in sawtimber trees that died in one year, between 1999 and 2003.

Average annual net growth of growing stock: The annual change in cubic-foot volume of sound wood in live sawtimber and poletimber trees, and the total volume of trees entering these classes through ingrowth less volume losses resulting from natural causes, between 1999 and 2003.

Average annual net growth of sawtimber: The annual change in the board-foot volume of live sawtimber trees, and the total volume of trees reaching sawtimber size less volume losses resulting from natural causes, between 1999 and 2003.

Average annual removals from growing stock: The average net growing-stock volume in growing-stock trees removed annually for roundwood forest products in addition to the volume of logging residues and the volume of other removals, between 1999 and 2003.

Average annual removals from sawtimber: The average net board-foot sawtimber volume of live sawtimber trees removed annually for roundwood forest products in addition to the volume of logging residues and the volume of other removals, between 1999 and 2003.

Basal area: Tree area in square feet of the cross section at breast height of a single tree. When the basal areas of all trees in a stand are summed, the result usually is expressed as square feet of basal area per acre.

Bioindicator species: A tree, woody shrub, or nonwoody herb species that responds to ambient levels of ozone pollution with distinct visible foliar symptoms that are easy to diagnose.

Biomass: The aboveground volume of live trees (including bark but excluding foliage) reported in green tons (i.e., green weight). Biomass has four components:

   Bole: Biomass of a tree from 1 foot above the ground to a 4-inch top outside bark.

   Tops and limbs: Total biomass of a tree from a 1-foot stump minus the bole.

   1- to 5-inch trees: Total aboveground biomass of a tree from 1 to 5 inches in d.b.h.

   Stump: Biomass of a tree 5 inches and larger in d.b.h. from the ground to a height of 1 foot.

Bulk density: The mass of soil per unit volume. A measure of the ratio of pore space to solid materials in a given soil. Expressed in units of grams per cubic centimeter of oven dry soil.

Commercial species: Tree species suitable for industrial wood products.

Compacted live-crown ratio: The percentage of the total length of the tree that supports a full, live crown. To determine compacted live crown ratio for trees with uneven length crowns, lower branches are transferred visually to fill holes in the upper portions of the crown until a full, even crown is created.

County and municipal: An ownership class of public lands owned by counties or local public agencies, or lands leased by these governmental units for more than 50 years.

Cropland: Land under cultivation within the last 24 months. Includes cropland harvested, crop failures, cultivated summer fallow, idle cropland used only for pasture, orchards, active Christmas tree plantations indicated by annual shearing, nurseries, and land in soil improvement crops, but excludes land cultivated in developing improved pasture.

Crown: The part of a tree or woody plant bearing live branches or foliage.

Crown dieback: Recent mortality of branches with fine twigs, which begins at the terminal portion of a branch and proceeds toward the trunk. Dieback is considered only when it occurs in the upper and outer portions of the tree. When whole branches are dead in the upper crown with no obvious signs of damage such as breaks or animal injury, it is assumed that the branches died from the terminal portion of the branch. Dead branches in the lower portion of the live crown are assumed to have died from competition and shading.

Cull tree: A live tree, 5 or larger in d.b.h., that is unmerchantable for saw logs now or prospectively due to rot, roughness, or species (see definitions for rotten and rough trees.).

Decay class: Qualitative assessment of stage of decay (five classes) of coarse woody debris based on visual assessments of color of wood, presence/absence of twigs and branches, texture of rotten portions, and structural integrity.

Diameter class: A classification of trees based on diameter outside bark (d.o.b.) measured at breast height (4.5 feet above the ground). D.b.h. is the common abbreviation for "diameter at breast height." With 2-inch diameter classes, the 6-inch class, for example, includes trees 5 to 6.9 inches in d.b.h.

Down woody material (DWM): Woody pieces of trees and shrubs that have been uprooted (no longer supporting growth) or severed from their root system, not self-supporting, and lying on the ground.

Duff: A soil layer dominated by organic material derived from the decomposition of plant and animal litter and deposited on an organic or a mineral surface. This layer is distinguished from the litter layer in that the original organic material has undergone sufficient decomposition that the source of this material (e.g., individual plant parts) no longer can be identified.

Effective cation exchange capacity (ECEC): The sum of cations that a soil can adsorb in its natural pH. Expressed in units of centimoles of positive charge per kilogram of soil.

Federal: An ownership class of public lands owned by the U.S. Government.

Fiber products: Products derived from wood and bark residues, for example, pulp, composition-board products, and wood chips for export.

Fine materials: Wood residues not suitable for chipping, for example, planer shavings and sawdust.

Fine woody debris (FWD): Dead branches, twigs, wood splinters 0.1 to 2.9 inches in diameter.

Forest industry: An ownership class of private lands owned by companies or individuals operating wood-using plants.

Forest land: Land at least 10-percent stocked by forest trees of any size, including land that formerly had such tree cover and that will be naturally or artificially regenerated. Forest land includes transition zones, for example, areas between heavily forested and nonforested lands that are at least 10-percent stocked with forest trees and forest areas adjacent to urban and built-up lands. Also included are pinyon-juniper and chaparral areas in the West and afforested areas. The minimum area for classification of forest land is 1 acre. Roadside, streamside, and shelterbelt strips of trees must have a crown width of at least 120 feet to qualify as forest land. Unimproved roads and trails, streams, and clearings in forest areas are classified as forest if less than 120 feet wide.

Forest type: A classification of forest land based on the species currently forming a plurality of the live-tree stocking.

Forest-type group: A combination of forest types that share closely associated species or site requirements and that generally are combined for brevity in reporting.

Major eastern forest-type groups:

   White/red/jack pine: Forests in which eastern white pine, red pine, or jack pine, singly or in combination, comprise a plurality of the stocking. Common associates include hemlock, aspen, birch, and maple.

Oak/pine: Forests in which hardwoods (usually upland oaks) comprise a plurality of the stocking but in which pine or eastern redcedar accounts for 25 to 50 percent of the stocking. Common associates include gum, hickory, and yellow-poplar.

Oak/hickory: Forests in which upland oaks or hickory, singly or in combination, comprise a plurality of the stocking except where pines account for 25 to 50 percent, in which case the stand is classified as oak-pine. Common associates include yellow-poplar, elm, maple, and black walnut.

Oak-gum/cypress: Bottomland forests in which tupelo, blackgum, sweetgum, oaks, or southern cypress, singly or in combination, comprise a plurality of the stocking except where pines account for 25 to 50 percent, in which case the stand is classified as oak-pine. Common associates include cottonwood, willow, ash, elm, hackberry, and maple.

Elm/ash/cottonwood: Forests in which elm, ash, or cottonwood, singly or in combination, comprise a plurality of the stocking. Common associates include willow, sycamore, beech, and maple.

Maple/beech/birch: Forests in which maple, beech, or yellow birch, singly or in combination, comprise a plurality of the stocking. Common associates include hemlock, elm, basswood, and white pine.

Aspen/birch: Forests in which aspen, balsam poplar, paper birch, or gray birch, singly or in combination, comprise a plurality of the stocking. Common associates include maple and balsam fir.

Growing stock: A classification of timber inventory that includes live trees of commercial species that meet specified standards of quality or vigor. Cull trees are excluded. When associated with volume, includes only trees 5 inches. and larger in d.b.h.

Hardwood: A dicotyledonous tree, usually broad-leaved and deciduous.

Industrial wood: All commercial roundwood products except fuelwood.

Land area: The area of dry land and land temporarily or partly covered by water, for example, marshes, swamps, and river flood plains; streams, sloughs, estuaries, and canals less than 200 feet wide; and lakes, reservoirs, and ponds less than 4.5 acres in area.

Litter: Undecomposed or only partially decomposed organic material that can be readily identified (e.g., plant leaves, twigs).

Live cull: A classification that includes live, cull trees. When associated with volume, it is the net volume in live, cull trees that are 5 inches and larger in d.b.h.

Log grade: A log classification based on external characteristics as indicators of quality or value. Also see Tree grade. (See USDA For. Serv. 2005 for information on tree-grading field techniques.)

Logging residues: The unused portions of growing-stock and nongrowing-stock trees cut or killed by logging and left in the woods.

Merchantable: Refers to a pulpwood or sawlog section that meets pulpwood or saw log specifications, respectively.

National forest: An ownership class of Federal lands, designated by Executive Order or statute as National Forests or purchase units, and other lands administered by the Forest Service; includes experimental areas.

Net annual growth: The average annual net increase in the volume of trees during the period between inventories. Components include the increment in net volume of trees at the beginning of the specific year surviving to its end, plus the net volume of trees reaching the minimum size class during the year, minus the volume of trees that died during the year, and minus the net volume of trees that became cull trees during the year.

Net volume in cubic feet: The gross volume in cubic feet less deductions for rot, roughness, and poor form. Volume is computed for the central stem, from a 1-foot stump to a minimum 4-inch top diameter outside bark (d.o.b.), or to the point where the central stem breaks into limbs.

Noncommercial species: Tree species of typically small size, poor form, or inferior quality that usually do not develop into trees suitable for industrial wood products.

Nonforest land: Land that has never supported forests and lands formerly forested where the use of timber management is precluded by development for other uses. (Includes area used for crops, improved pasture, residential areas, city parks, improved roads of any width and adjoining clearings, powerline clearings of any width, and 1- to 4.5-acre areas of water classified by the Bureau of the Census as land. If intermingled in forest areas, unimproved roads and nonforest strips must be more than 120 feet wide, and clearings, etc. must be more than 1 acre in area to qualify as nonforest land.)

Nonindustrial private: An ownership class of private lands such that the owner does not operate wood-using plants.

Nonstocked areas: Timberland less than 10-percent stocked with live trees.

Other red oaks: A group of species in the genus *Quercus* that includes scarlet oak, northern pin oak, southern red oak, bear oak, shingle oak, laurel oak, blackjack oak, water oak, pin oak, willow oak, and black oak.

Other white oaks: A group of species in the genus *Quercus* that includes overcup oak, chestnut oak, and post oak.

Ownership: The property owned by one ownership unit, including all parcels of land in the United States.

Ownership unit: A classification of ownership encompassing all types of legal entities with an ownership interest in land regardless of the number of people involved. A unit can be an individual; combination of persons; legal entity such as a corporation, partnership, club, or trust; or public agency. An ownership unit has control of a parcel or group of parcels of land.

Ozone: A regional, gaseous air pollutant produced primarily through sunlight-driven chemical reactions of nitrogen dioxide and hydrocarbons in the atmosphere and causing foliar injury to deciduous trees, conifers, shrubs, and herbaceous species.

Ozone bioindicator site: An open area used for ozone injury evaluations on ozone-sensitive species. The area must meet certain site selection guidelines on size, condition, and plant counts to be used for evaluations of ozone injury in FIA.

Physiographic class: A measure of soil and water conditions that affect tree growth on a site. The physiographic classes are:

> *Xeric*: Very dry soils where excessive drainage seriously limits both growth and species occurrence. These sites usually are on upland and upper half slopes.

> *Xeromesic*: Moderately dry soils where excessive drainage limits growth and species occurrence to some extent. These sites usually are on the lower half slopes.

> *Mesic*: Deep, well drained soils. Growth and species occurrence are limited only by climate. These include all cove sites and bottomlands along intermittent streams.

> *Hydromesic*: Moderately wet soils where insufficient drainage or infrequent flooding limits growth and species occurrence to some extent.

> *Hydric*: Very wet sites where excess water seriously limits both growth and species occurrence.

Poletimber trees: Live trees at least 5 inches in d.b.h. but smaller than sawtimber trees.

Primary wood-using mill: A mill that converts roundwood products into other wood products. Common examples are sawmills that convert saw logs into lumber and pulpmills that convert pulpwood into wood pulp.

Productivity class: A classification of forest land in terms of potential annual cubic-foot volume growth per acre at culmination of mean annual increment in fully stocked natural stands.

Pulpwood: Roundwood, whole-tree chips, or wood residues used for the production of wood pulp.

Reserved forest land: Forest land withdrawn from timber utilization through statute, administrative regulation, or designation without regard to productive status.

Residues: Bark and woody materials that are generated in primary wood-using mills when roundwood products are converted to other products. Examples are slabs, edgings, trimmings, miscuts, sawdust, shavings, veneer cores and clippings, and pulp screenings. Includes bark residues and wood residues (both coarse and fine materials) but excludes logging residues.

Rotten tree: A live tree of commercial species that does not contain a saw log now or prospectively primarily because of rot (that is, when rot accounts for more than 50 percent of the total cull volume).

Rough tree: (a) A live tree of commercial species that does not contain a saw log now or prospectively primarily because of roughness (that is, when sound cull due to such factors as poor form, splits, or cracks accounts for more than 50 percent of the total cull volume) or (b) a live tree of noncommercial species.

Roundwood products: Logs, bolts, and other round timber generated from harvesting trees for industrial or consumer use.

Salvable dead tree: A downed or standing dead tree considered currently or potentially merchantable by regional standards.

Saplings: Live trees 1.0 through 4.9 inches in d.b.h.

Saw log: A log meeting minimum standards of diameter, length, and defect, including logs at least 8 feet long, sound and straight, and with a minimum diameter inside bark (d.i.b.) of 6 inches for softwoods and 8 inches for hardwoods, or meeting other combinations of size and defect specified by regional standards.

Sawtimber tree: A live tree of commercial species containing at least a 12-foot sawlog or two noncontiguous saw logs 8 feet or longer, and meeting regional specifications for freedom from defect. Softwoods must be at least 9 inches in d.b.h. Hardwoods must be at least 11 inches in d.b.h.

Sawtimber volume: Net volume of the saw-log portion of live sawtimber in board feet, International 1/4-inch rule (unless specified otherwise), from stump to a minimum 7 inches top d.o.b. for softwoods and a minimum 9 inches top d.o.b. for hardwoods.

Seedlings: Live trees less than 1 inch in d.b.h. and at least 1 foot tall.

Select red oaks: A group of species in the genus *Quercus* that includes cherrybark oak, northern red oak, and Shumard oak.

Select white oaks: A group of species in the genus *Quercus* that includes white oak, swamp white oak, bur oak, swamp chestnut oak, and chinkapin oak.

Site index: An expression of forest-site quality based on the height of a free-growing dominant or codominant tree of a representative species in the forest type at age 50.

Snag: A standing dead tree. In the current inventory, a snag must be 5 inches in d.b.h. and 4.5 feet tall, and have a lean angle less than 45 degrees from vertical. A snag can be self-supported by its roots or supported by another tree or snag.

Softwood: A coniferous tree, usually evergreen, with needles or scale-like leaves.

Sound dead: The net volume in salvable dead trees.

Stand: A group of trees on a minimum of 1 acre of forest land that is stocked by forest trees of any size.

Stand-size class: A classification of forest land based on the size class of live trees in the area. The classes include:

> *Nonstocked*: Forest land stocked with less than 10 percent of full stocking with live trees. Examples are recently cutover areas or recently reverted agricultural fields.

> *Seedling-sapling*: Forest land stocked with at least 10 percent of full stocking with live trees with half or more of such stocking in seedlings or saplings, or both.

> *Poletimber*: Forest land stocked with at least 10 percent of full stocking with live trees with half or more of such stocking in poletimber or sawtimber trees or both, and in which the stocking of poletimber exceeds that of sawtimber.

> *Sawtimber*: Forest land stocked with at least 10 percent of full stocking with live trees with half or more of such stocking in poletimber or sawtimber trees, or both, and in which the stocking of sawtimber is at least equal to that of poletimber.

State: An ownership class of public lands owned by states or lands leased by states for more than 50 years.

Stocking: The degree of occupancy of land by trees, measured by basal area or number of trees by size and spacing, or both, compared to a stocking standard; that is, the basal area or number of trees, or both, required to fully utilize the growth potential of the land.

Timberland: Forest land that is producing or is capable of producing crops of industrial wood and not withdrawn from timber utilization by statute or administrative regulation. Areas qualifying as timberland are capable of producing in excess of 20 cubic feet per acre per year of industrial wood in natural stands. Includes currently inaccessible and inoperable.

Timber products output: All timber products cut from roundwood and byproducts of wood manufacturing plants. Roundwood products include logs, bolts, or other round sections cut from growing-stock trees, cull trees, salvable dead trees, trees on nonforest land, noncommercial species, sapling-size trees, and limbwood. Byproducts from primary manufacturing plants include slabs, edging, trimmings, miscuts, sawdust, shavings, veneer cores and clippings, and screenings of pulpmills that are used as pulpwood chips or other products.

Tree: A woody plant usually having one or more erect perennial stems, a stem d.b.h. of at least 3 inches, a more or less definitely formed crown of foliage, and a height of at least 13 feet at maturity.

Tree size class: A classification of trees based on diameter at breast height, including sawtimber trees, poletimber trees, saplings, and seedlings.

Tops: The wood of a tree above the merchantable height (or above the point on the stem 4 inches d.o.b.) ; includes the usable material in the uppermost stem.

Urban forest land: Land that otherwise would meet criteria for timberland but is in an urban-suburban area surrounded by commercial, industrial, or residential development and unlikely to be managed for the production of industrial wood products on a continuing basis. Wood removed would be for land clearing, fuelwood, or esthetic purposes. Such forest land may be associated with industrial, commercial, residential subdivision, industrial parks, golf course perimeters, airport buffer strips, and public urban parks that qualify as forest land.

Unreserved forest land: Forest land not withdrawn from harvest by statute or administrative regulation. Includes forest lands that are not capable of producing in excess of 20 cubic feet per acre per year of industrial wood in natural stands.

Veneer log: A roundwood product from which veneer is sliced or sawn and that usually meets certain standards of minimum diameter and length and maximum defect.

Weight: The weight of wood and bark, oven-dry basis (approximately 0-percent moisture content).

LITERATURE CITED

Bechtold, W.A.; Patterson, P.L., eds. 2005. **The enhanced Forest Inventory and Analysis program—national sampling design and estimation procedures.** Gen. Tech. Rep. SRS-80. Asheville, NC: U.S. Department of Agriculture, Forest Service, Southern Research Station. 85 p.

Brand, G.J.; Nelson, M.D.; Wendt, D.G.; Nimerfro, K.K. 2000. **The hexagon/panel system for selecting FIA plots under an annual inventory.** In: McRoberts, R.E.; Reams, G.A.; Van Deusen, P.C., eds., Proceedings of the first annual Forest Inventory and Analysis symposium. Gen. Tech. Rep. NC-213. St. Paul, MN: U.S. Department of Agriculture, Forest Service, Northern Research Station: 8-13.

DellaSala, D.A.; Staus, N.L.; Strittholt, J.R.; Hackman, A.; Iacobelli, A. 2001. **An updated protected areas database for the United States and Canada.** Natural Areas Journal. 21(2): 124-135.

Gansner, D.A. 1965. **Missouri's forests, 1959.** Resour. Bull. CS-2. Columbus, OH: U.S. Department of Agriculture, Forest Service, Central States Forest Experiment Station. 53 p.

Hahn, J.T.; Hansen, M.H. 1991. **Cubic and board foot volume models for the Central States.** Northern Journal of Applied Forestry. 8: 47-57.

Hansen. M.H.; Wendt, D.G. 2000. **Using classified Landsat Thematic Mapper data for stratification in a statewide forest inventory.** In: McRoberts, R.E.; Reams, G.A.; Van Deusen, P.C., eds. Proceedings of the first annual Forest Inventory and Analysis symposium. Gen. Tech. Rep. NC-213. St. Paul, MN: U.S. Department of Agriculture, Forest Service, Northern Research Station: 20-27.

McRoberts, R.E. 1999. **Joint annual forest inventory and monitoring system: the North Central perspective.** Journal of Forestry. 97: 21-26.

McRoberts, R.E.; Wendt, D.G.; Nelson, M.D.; and Hansen, M.H.. 2002. **Using a land cover classification based on satellite imagery to improve the precision of forest inventory area estimates.** Remote Sensing of the Environment. 80: 1-9.

McRoberts, R.E. 2003. **Compensating for missing plot observations in forest inventory estimation.** Canadian Journal of Forest Research. 33: 1990-1997.

McRoberts, R.E. 2005. **Overview of the enhanced forest inventory and analysis program.** In: Bechtold, W.A.; Patterson, P. L., eds. The enhanced forest inventory and analysis program—national sampling design and estimation procedures. Gen. Tech. Rep. SRS-80. Asheville, NC: U.S. Department of Agriculture, Forest Service, Southern Research Station: 1-10.

Spencer, J.S., Jr.; Essex, B.L. 1976. **Timber in Missouri, 1972.** Resour. Bull. NC-30. St. Paul, MN: U.S. Department of Agriculture, Forest Service, North Central Forest Experiment Station. 108 p.

Spencer, J.S., Roussopoulous, S.M.; Massengale, R.A. 1992. **Missouri's forest resource, 1989: an analysis.** Resour. Bull. NC-139. St. Paul, MN: U.S. Department of Agriculture, Forest Service, North Central Forest Experiment Station. 84 p.

U.S. Department of Agriculture, Forest Service. 1948. **Forest resources of Missouri, 1947.** For. Surv. Rel. 6. Columbus, OH: U.S. Department of Agriculture, Forest Service, Central States Forest Experiment Station 19 p.

U.S. Department of Agriculture, Forest Service. 2005. **Forest Inventory and /analysis national core field guide; Volume 1: field data collection procedures for Phase 2 plots, ver. 3.0.** Washington, DC: U.S. Department of Agriculture, Forest Service. Available at www.fia.fs.fed.us/library/field-guides-methods-proc.

Vogelmann, J.E.; Howard, S.M.; Yang, L.; Larson, C.R.; Wylie, B.K.; Van Driel, N. 2001. **Completion of the 1990s National Land Cover Data Set for the conterminous United States from Landsat Thematic Mapper data and ancillary data sources.** Photogrammetric Engineering and Remote Sensing. 67: 650-662.

Woodall, C.W.; Williams, M.S. 2005. **Sampling, estimation, and analysis procedures for the down woody materials indicator.** Gen. Tech. Rep. NC-256. St. Paul, MN: U.S. Department of Agriculture, Forest Service, North Central Research Station. 47 p.

TABLES

Table A.—Area and number of plots in each stratum for the stratification used by NRS-FIA for estimation in Missouri, 1999-2003

Table B.—State-level estimates of major forest resource attributes and their sampling errors

Table C.—Percent compliance to measurement quality objectives (MQO) tolerances of variables for blind check plots measured over 1999-2003

Table D.—Observed relative bias values (average [field crew - QA crew]) for blind check plots measured over 1999-2003

Table E.—FIA nonresponse by strata for annual inventories measured in 1999-2003

FOREST-ATTRIBUTE TABLES FOR MISSOURI
Area

Table 1.—Percentage of area by land status
Table 2.—Area of accessible forest land by owner class and forest-land status
Table 3.—Area of accessible forest land by forest-type group and productivity class
Table 4.—Area of accessible forest land by forest-type group, ownership group, and land status
Table 5.—Area of accessible forest land by forest-type group and stand-size class
Table 6.—Area of accessible forest land by forest-type group and stand-age class
Table 7.—Area of accessible forest land by forest-type group and stand origin
Table 8.—Area of accessible forest land disturbed annually by forest-type group and disturbance class
Table 9.—Area of timberland by forest-type group and stand-size class

Number

Table 10.—Number of live trees on forest land by species group and diameter class
Table 11.—Number of growing-stock trees on timberland by species group and diameter class

Volume

Table 12.—Net volume of live trees by owner class and forest land status
Table 13.—Net volume of live trees on forest land by forest-type group and stand-size class
Table 14.—Net volume of live trees on forest land by species group and ownership group
Table 15.—Net volume of live trees on forest land by species group and diameter class
Table 16.—Net volume of live trees on accessible forest land by forest-type group and stand origin
Table 17.—Net volume of growing-stock trees on timberland by species group and diameter class
Table 18.—Net volume of growing-stock trees on timberland by species group and ownership group
Table 19.—Net volume of sawtimber trees (International ¼-inch rule) on timberland by species group and diameter class

Table 19a.—Net volume of sawtimber trees (Doyle rule) on timberland by species group and diameter class

Table 20.—Net volume of sawtimber trees on timberland by species group and ownership group

Growth, Mortality, and Removals

Table 24.—Average annual net growth of growing-stock trees on timberland by species group and ownership group, 1998 to 1999-2003

Table 28.—Average annual mortality of growing-stock trees on timberland by species group and ownership group, 1998 to 1999-2003

Table 30.—Average annual removals of growing-stock trees on timberland by species group and ownership group, 1998 to 1999-2003

Weight

Table 31.—Aboveground dry weight of live trees by owner class and forest-land status

Table 32.—Aboveground dry weight of live trees on forest land by species group and diameter class

County-Level

Table 54.—Area of accessible forest land by Forest Survey Unit, county, and forest land status

Table 55.—Area of accessible forest land by Forest Survey Unit, county, ownership group, and forest land status

Table 56.—Area of accessible forest land by Forest Survey Unit, county/county group, and forest type group

Table 57.—Area of timberland by Forest Survey Unit, county, and stand-size class

Table 58.—Area of timberland by Forest Survey Unit, county, and stocking class

Table 59.—Net volume of growing stock and sawtimber (International ¼-rule) on timberland by Forest Survey Unit, county, and major species group

Table 59a.—Net volume of growing stock and sawtimber (Doyle rule) on timberland by Forest Survey Unit, county, and major species group

Table 60.—Average annual net growth of growing stock and sawtimber (International ¼-rule) on timberland by Forest Survey Unit, county, and major species group

Table 60a.—Average annual net growth of growing stock and sawtimber (Doyle rule) on timberland by Forest Survey Unit, county, and major species group

Table 61.—Average annual removals of growing stock and sawtimber (International ¼-rule) on timberland by Forest Survey Unit, county, and major species group

Table 61a.—Average annual removals of growing stock and sawtimber (Doyle rule) on timberland by Forest Survey Unit, county, and major species group

*All tables contain forest attribute estimates for Missouri for measurements taken from 1999 to 2003, except where indicated

**Gaps in enumeration of tables are placeholders for future reports where tables may be available, but at this time are unavailable due to estimation limitations with new annual inventory design (i.e., growth, removal, and mortality tables).

Table A.—Area and number of plots in each stratum for the stratification used by NRS-FIA for estimation in Missouri, 1999-2003 (unshaded rows are the strata used in estimation, shaded rows are summaries)

Unit-County[a]	Ownership layer[b]	Classified NLCD layer[c]	Area (Acres)[d]	Selected[e]	Nonforest office plots[f]	Field check plots[g]	Field check plots measured[h]	Forest plots measured[i]	Forest plots measured for change[j]	Plots not measured[k]
1-3 & 5	USFS	Forest	1,441,000	410	2	408	406	405	169	2
1-3 & 5	USFS	Forest edge	46,000	8	0	8	8	8	2	0
1-3 & 5	USFS	Nonfor. & nonfor. edge	23,000	10	4	6	6	5	2	0
1-3 & 5	USFS		1,510,000	428	6	422	420	418	173	2
1	Other public	Nonforest	14,000	5	5	0	0	0		0
1	Other public	Nonforest edge	21,000	6	3	3	3	2	1	0
1	Other public	Forest	397,000	126	0	126	124	123	30	2
1	Other public	Forest edge	32,000	9	1	8	8	8	2	0
1	Other public		464,000	146	9	137	135	133	33	2
2	Other public	Nonfor. & nonfor. edge	53,000	8	7	1	1	1	1	0
2	Other public	Forest - forest edge	77,000	12	0	12	12	12	7	0
2	Other public		130,000	20	7	13	13	13	8	0
3	Other public	Nonfor. & nonfor. edge	45,000	7	4	3	3	1	0	0
3	Other public	Forest - forest edge	78,000	13	1	12	12	12	6	0
3	Other public		123,000	20	5	15	15	13	6	0
4	Other public	Nonforest	145,000	25	24	1	1	1	0	0
4	Other public	Nonforest edge	98,000	12	4	8	8	8	6	0
4	Other public	Forest	85,000	13	0	13	13	13	9	0
4	Other public	Forest edge	93,000	13	3	10	10	10	5	0
4	Other public		421,000	63	31	32	32	32	20	0
5	Other public	Nonforest	33,000	9	8	1	1	1	0	0
5	Other public	Nonforest edge	27,000	10	5	5	5	3	2	0
5	Other public	Forest	89,000	30	1	29	28	26	12	1
5	Other public	Forest edge	31,000	15	2	13	12	11	1	1
5	Other public		180,000	64	16	48	46	41	15	2
All units	All Public		2,828,000	741	74	667	661	650	255	6

- - - Public Lands - - -

26

Table A.—continued

Unit-County[a]	Ownership layer[b]	Classified NLCD layer[c]	Area (Acres)[d]	Selected[e]	Nonforest office plots[f]	Field check plots[g]	Field check plots measured[h]	Forest plots measured[i]	Forest plots measured for change[j]	Plots not measured[k]
								Number of plots		
- Private Lands- Unit 1 -										
Bollinger	Private	Nonforest	79,000	24	22	2	2	1	0	0
Bollinger	Private	Nonforest edge	78,000	27	10	17	15	14	6	2
Bollinger	Private	Forest	146,000	43	0	43	37	36	11	6
Bollinger	Private	Forest edge	79,000	19	3	16	15	15	9	1
			382,000	113	35	78	69	66	26	9
Butler	Private	Nonforest	216,000	57	57	0	0	0	0	0
Butler	Private	Nonforest edge	53,000	24	16	8	8	2	0	0
Butler	Private	Forest	72,000	28	1	27	23	23	8	4
Butler	Private	Forest edge	45,000	12	2	10	9	9	1	1
			386,000	121	76	45	40	34	9	5
Crawford	Private	Nonforest	33,000	10	9	1	1	0	0	0
Crawford	Private	Nonforest edge	66,000	25	16	9	8	4	2	1
Crawford	Private	Forest	234,000	65	1	64	56	56	21	8
Crawford	Private	Forest edge	82,000	28	8	20	19	14	6	1
			415,000	128	34	94	84	74	29	10
Dent	Private	Nonforest	64,000	16	16	0	0	0	0	0
Dent	Private	Nonforest edge	68,000	18	7	11	10	6	2	1
Dent	Private	Forest	184,000	63	2	61	50	48	23	11
Dent	Private	Forest edge	73,000	23	5	18	15	9	3	3
			389,000	120	30	90	75	63	28	15
Iron	Private	Nonforest	16,000	6	6	0	0	0	0	0
Iron	Private	Nonforest edge	25,000	4	2	2	2	2	0	0
Iron	Private	Forest	173,000	65	0	65	58	58	22	7
Iron	Private	Forest edge	30,000	7	1	6	6	5	2	0
			244,000	82	9	73	66	65	24	7
Madison	Private	Nonforest	28,000	8	8	0	0	0	0	0
Madison	Private	Nonforest edge	34,000	8	5	3	3	1		0
Madison	Private	Forest	163,000	48	2	46	41	41	18	5
Madison	Private	Forest edge	38,000	11	2	9	8	8	2	1
			263,000	75	17	58	52	50	20	6
Oregon	Private	Nonforest	61,000	13	9	4	4	1	0	0
Oregon	Private	Nonforest edge	78,000	23	12	11	10	6	4	1
Oregon	Private	Forest	179,000	62	3	59	51	48	21	8
Oregon	Private	Forest edge	82,000	26	6	20	18	11	4	2
			400,000	124	30	94	83	66	29	11
Ripley	Private	Nonforest	49,000	17	17	0	0	0	0	0
Ripley	Private	Nonforest edge	51,000	16	9	7	6	3	1	1
Ripley	Private	Forest	143,000	44	3	41	39	39	12	2
Ripley	Private	Forest edge	55,000	18	3	15	11	10	4	4
			298,000	95	32	63	56	52	17	7
St. Francois	Private	Nonforest	52,000	14	14	0	0	0	0	0
St. Francois	Private	Nonforest edge	51,000	12	5	7	7	3	0	0
St. Francois	Private	Forest	122,000	38	0	38	33	33	15	5
St. Francois	Private	Forest edge	51,000	14	2	12	12	9	4	0
			276,000	78	21	57	52	45	19	5
Shannon	Private	Nonforest	32,000	8	8	0	0	0	0	0
Shannon	Private	Nonforest edge	39,000	13	6	7	7	4	1	0
Shannon	Private	Forest	269,000	76	0	76	72	72	34	4
Shannon	Private	Forest edge	46,000	20	2	18	16	11	3	2
			386,000	117	16	101	95	87	38	6
Washington	Private	Nonforest	20,000	6	4	2	2	0	0	0
Washington	Private	Nonforest edge	41,000	20	12	8	8	5	2	0
Washington	Private	Forest	276,000	78	2	76	65	63	30	11
Washington	Private	Forest edge	54,000	15	1	14	12	10	5	2
			391,000	119	19	100	87	78	37	13
Wayne	Private	Nonforest	23,000	6	4	2	2	0		0
Wayne	Private	Nonforest edge	37,000	11	6	5	5	4	2	0
Wayne	Private	Forest	221,000	73	0	73	64	64	27	9
Wayne	Private	Forest edge	44,000	11	2	9	8	6	4	1
			325,000	101	12	89	79	74	33	10
Carter & Reynolds	Private	Nonforest	21,000	8	8	0	0	0	0	0
Carter & Reynolds	Private	Nonforest edge	43,000	9	5	4	4	1	0	0
Carter & Reynolds	Private	Forest	443,000	128	3	125	112	111	34	13
Carter & Reynolds	Private	Forest edge	56,000	19	2	17	16	13	4	1
			563,000	164	18	146	132	125	38	14
Unit 1 all co.	Private	Total	4,718,000	1,437	349	1,088	970	879	347	118

Unit-County[a]	Ownership layer[b]	Classified NLCD layer[c]	Area (Acres)[d]	Number of plots						
				Selected[e]	Nonforest office plots[f]	Field check plots[g]	Field check plots measured[h]	Forest plots measured[i]	Forest plots measured for change[j]	Plots not measured[k]
- Private Lands- Unit 2- -										
Barry	Private	Nonforest	190,000	31	30	1	1	0	0	0
Barry	Private	Nonforest edge	85,000	11	4	7	6	4	1	1
Barry	Private	Forest	86,000	13	0	13	13	13	9	0
Barry	Private	Forest edge	72,000	18	3	15	14	13	8	1
			433,000	73	37	36	34	30	18	2
Christian	Private	Nonforest	124,000	23	22	1	1	1	1	0
Christian	Private	Nonforest edge	66,000	8	3	5	5	4	2	0
Christian	Private	Forest	61,000	10	0	10	10	8	5	0
Christian	Private	Forest edge	55,000	8	1	7	6	5	1	1
			306,000	49	26	23	22	18	9	1
Douglas	Private	Nonforest	78,000	9	8	1	1	1	0	0
Douglas	Private	Nonforest edge	104,000	25	7	18	17	15	9	1
Douglas	Private	Forest	187,000	31	0	31	29	28	23	2
Douglas	Private	Forest edge	109,000	14	1	13	12	9	5	1
			478,000	79	16	63	59	53	37	4
Howell	Private	Nonforest	126,000	23	20	3	3	2	2	0
Howell	Private	Nonforest edge	122,000	20	12	8	8	4	2	0
Howell	Private	Forest	174,000	26	1	25	24	24	21	1
Howell	Private	Forest edge	115,000	17	4	13	13	10	9	0
			537,000	86	37	49	48	40	34	1
McDonald	Private	Nonforest	84,000	13	13	0	0	0	0	0
McDonald	Private	Nonforest edge	71,000	8	4	4	4	3	2	0
McDonald	Private	Forest	119,000	24	0	24	24	23	17	0
McDonald	Private	Forest edge	67,000	14	2	12	10	9	8	2
			341,000	59	19	40	38	35	27	2
Newton	Private	Nonforest	196,000	34	29	5	5	3	1	0
Newton	Private	Nonforest edge	80,000	16	3	13	12	8	4	1
Newton	Private	Forest	58,000	8	0	8	8	8	7	0
Newton	Private	Forest edge	64,000	7	3	4	4	4	3	0
			398,000	65	35	30	29	23	15	1
Ozark	Private	Nonforest	68,000	10	7	3	3	2	1	0
Ozark	Private	Nonforest edge	80,000	17	10	7	7	5	5	0
Ozark	Private	Forest	196,000	31	0	31	28	25	21	3
Ozark	Private	Forest edge	85,000	16	3	13	13	11	8	0
			429,000	74	20	54	51	43	35	3
Stone	Private	Nonforest	57,000	6	6	0	0	0	0	0
Stone	Private	Nonforest edge	58,000	10	6	4	4	2	2	0
Stone	Private	Forest	93,000	15	0	15	15	14	11	0
Stone	Private	Forest edge	59,000	13	2	11	11	11	4	0
			267,000	44	14	30	30	27	17	0
Taney	Private	Nonforest	35,000	5	4	1	1	1	1	0
Taney	Private	Nonforest edge	60,000	7	4	3	3	2	2	0
Taney	Private	Forest	171,000	35	0	35	32	31	25	3
Taney	Private	Forest edge	72,000	11	0	11	11	11	8	0
			338,000	58	8	50	47	45	36	3
Texas	Private	Nonforest	143,000	22	21	1	1	0	0	0
Texas	Private	Nonforest edge	130,000	17	8	9	9	4	3	0
Texas	Private	Forest	286,000	50	2	48	45	44	34	3
Texas	Private	Forest edge	132,000	28	2	26	25	24	17	1
			691,000	117	33	84	80	72	54	4
Webster	Private	Nonforest	119,000	21	20	1	1	0	0	0
Webster	Private	Nonforest edge	100,000	13	6	7	7	5	3	0
Webster	Private	Forest	75,000	11	0	11	11	11	7	0
Webster	Private	Forest edge	84,000	13	3	10	10	10	9	0
			378,000	58	29	29	29	26	19	0
Wright	Private	Nonforest	99,000	23	18	5	5	1	0	0
Wright	Private	Nonforest edge	108,000	14	4	10	9	6	4	1
Wright	Private	Forest	120,000	22	1	21	21	20	14	0
Wright	Private	Forest edge	102,000	12	2	10	9	8	5	1
			325,000	101	12	89	79	74	33	10
Unit 2 all co.	Private	Total	5,025,000	833	299	534	511	447	324	23

28

Table A.—continued

Unit-County[a]	Ownership layer[b]	Classified NLCD layer[c]	Area (Acres)[d]	Number of plots						
				Selected[e]	Nonforest office plots[f]	Field check plots[g]	Field check plots measured[h]	Forest plots measured[i]	Forest plots measured for change[j]	Plots not measured[k]

Unit-County[a]	Ownership layer[b]	Classified NLCD layer[c]	Area (Acres)[d]	Selected[e]	Nonforest office plots[f]	Field check plots[g]	Field check plots measured[h]	Forest plots measured[i]	Forest plots measured for change[j]	Plots not measured[k]
- Private Lands- Unit 3 -										
Benton	Private	Nonforest	133,000	24	24	0	0	0	0	0
Benton	Private	Nonforest edge	74,000	7	5	2	2	0	0	0
Benton	Private	Forest	191,000	36	2	34	33	33	24	1
Benton	Private	Forest edge	79,000	13	1	12	11	11	11	1
			477,000	80	32	48	46	44	35	2
Camden	Private	Nonforest	48,000	7	7	0	0	0	0	0
Camden	Private	Nonforest edge	68,000	13	9	4	4	4	4	0
Camden	Private	Forest	236,000	30	0	30	28	28	21	2
Camden	Private	Forest edge	82,000	22	5	17	17	14	13	0
			434,000	72	21	51	49	46	38	2
Cedar	Private	Nonforest	116,000	19	16	3	3	1	1	0
Cedar	Private	Nonforest edge	67,000	16	7	9	9	7	5	0
Cedar	Private	Forest	51,000	4	0	4	4	4	4	0
Cedar	Private	Forest edge	56,000	10	1	9	8	8	4	1
			290,000	49	24	25	24	20	14	1
Dallas	Private	Nonforest	94,000	18	18	0	0	0	0	0
Dallas	Private	Nonforest edge	77,000	11	3	8	8	7	6	0
Dallas	Private	Forest	98,000	14	0	14	14	14	9	0
Dallas	Private	Forest edge	70,000	14	3	11	9	8	5	2
			339,000	57	24	33	31	29	20	2
Hickory	Private	Nonforest	59,000	6	6	0	0	0	0	0
Hickory	Private	Nonforest edge	44,000	12	7	5	4	2	2	1
Hickory	Private	Forest	98,000	15	0	15	12	12	7	3
Hickory	Private	Forest edge	46,000	9	3	6	6	6	5	0
			247,000	42	16	26	22	20	14	4
Laclede	Private	Nonforest	112,000	17	15	2	1	1	1	1
Laclede	Private	Nonforest edge	105,000	19	11	8	7	5	4	1
Laclede	Private	Forest	141,000	26	1	25	25	24	19	0
Laclede	Private	Forest edge	99,000	15	2	13	13	13	11	0
			457,000	77	29	48	46	43	35	2
Maries	Private	Nonforest	59,000	15	15	0	0	0	0	0
Maries	Private	Nonforest edge	79,000	10	3	7	6	3	3	1
Maries	Private	Forest	116,000	22	2	20	19	19	17	1
Maries	Private	Forest edge	83,000	8	1	7	6	6	4	1
			337,000	55	21	34	31	28	24	3
Miller	Private	Nonforest	66,000	12	12	0	0	0	0	0
Miller	Private	Nonforest edge	83,000	18	5	13	12	8	2	1
Miller	Private	Forest	133,000	13	0	13	12	12	10	1
Miller	Private	Forest edge	88,000	17	0	17	15	14	13	2
			370,000	60	17	43	39	34	25	4
Morgan	Private	Nonforest	100,000	18	18	0	0	0	0	0
Morgan	Private	Nonforest edge	61,000	11	6	5	3	3	1	2
Morgan	Private	Forest	169,000	27	1	26	24	24	15	2
Morgan	Private	Forest edge	60,000	11	3	8	8	7	4	0
			390,000	67	28	39	35	34	20	4
Phelps	Private	Nonforest	49,000	7	5	2	2	0	0	0
Phelps	Private	Nonforest edge	75,000	8	7	1	1	1	0	0
Phelps	Private	Forest	158,000	30	0	30	27	27	24	3
Phelps	Private	Forest edge	84,000	19	5	14	13	10	6	1
			366,000	64	17	47	43	38	30	4
Polk	Private	Nonforest	177,000	27	25	2	2	0	0	0
Polk	Private	Nonforest edge	98,000	18	14	4	4	4	3	0
Polk	Private	Forest	51,000	9	0	9	9	8	7	0
Polk	Private	Forest edge	73,000	14	3	11	9	9	7	2
			399,000	68	42	26	24	21	17	2
Pulaski	Private	Nonforest	30,000	6	6	0	0	0	0	0
Pulaski	Private	Nonforest edge	57,000	9	3	6	5	4	4	1
Pulaski	Private	Forest	147,000	29	1	28	23	21	18	5
Pulaski	Private	Forest edge	70,000	12	4	8	6	5	3	2
			304,000	56	14	42	34	30	25	8
St. Clair	Private	Nonforest	155,000	22	20	2	2	1	0	0
St. Clair	Private	Nonforest edge	83,000	13	9	4	4	3	3	0
St. Clair	Private	Forest	131,000	22	0	22	21	21	17	1
St. Clair	Private	Forest edge	74,000	17	3	14	13	8	7	1
			443,000	74	32	42	40	33	27	2
Unit 3 all co.	Private	Total	4,853,000	821	317	504	464	420	324	40

29

Unit-County[a]	Ownership layer[b]	Classified NLCD layer[c]	Area (Acres)[d]	Selected[e]	Nonforest office plots[f]	Field check plots[g]	Field check plots measured[h]	Forest plots measured[i]	Forest plots measured for change[j]	Plots not measured[k]
								Number of plots		
---	---	---	---	---	-Private Lands- Unit 4-	---	---	---	---	---
4A	Private	Nonforest	1,462,000	237	222	15	14	5	2	1
4A	Private	Nonforest edge	487,000	74	38	36	31	18	12	5
4A	Private	Forest	155,000	35	1	34	33	32	24	1
4A	Private	Forest edge	307,000	57	21	36	35	32	23	1
			2,411,000	403	282	121	113	87	61	8
4B	Private	Nonforest	1,704,000	268	248	20	18	5	4	2
4B	Private	Nonforest edge	567,000	103	53	50	48	38	28	2
4B	Private	Forest	141,000	31	1	30	28	27	23	2
4B	Private	Forest edge	352,000	66	9	57	54	49	35	3
			2,764,000	468	311	157	148	119	90	9
4NC	Private	Nonforest	1,517,000	259	245	14	14	4	2	0
4NC	Private	Nonforest edge	813,000	131	80	51	45	23	17	6
4NC	Private	Forest	142,000	19	2	17	15	15	9	2
4NC	Private	Forest edge	488,000	82	20	62	56	48	39	6
			2,960,000	491	347	144	130	90	67	14
4NE	Private	Nonforest	1,793,000	312	301	11	11	2	2	0
4NE	Private	Nonforest edge	997,000	153	106	47	42	29	23	5
4NE	Private	Forest	307,000	58	1	57	51	49	42	6
4NE	Private	Forest edge	688,000	124	38	86	82	73	54	4
			3,785,000	647	446	201	186	153	121	15
4NW	Private	Nonforest	2,215,000	375	357	18	17	3	2	1
4NW	Private	Nonforest edge	857,000	142	94	48	44	29	23	4
4NW	Private	Forest	67,000	14	1	13	12	12	9	1
4NW	Private	Forest edge	430,000	66	18	48	46	39	32	2
			3,569,000	597	470	127	119	83	66	8
4RIV	Private	Nonforest	2,584,000	445	424	21	20	7	5	1
4RIV	Private	Nonforest edge	688,000	123	73	50	47	33	23	3
4RIV	Private	Forest	98,000	16	1	15	14	14	12	1
4RIV	Private	Forest edge	381,000	52	11	41	38	36	25	3
			1,462,000	237	222	15	14	5	2	1
Unit 4 all co.	Private	Total	19,240,000	3,242	2,365	877	815	622	470	62
---	---	---	---	---	-Private Lands- Unit 5-	---	---	---	---	---
Boone	Private	Nonforest	172,000	51	50	1	1	1	0	0
Boone	Private	Nonforest edge	108,000	34	18	16	15	9	4	1
Boone	Private	Forest	63,000	20	1	19	18	17	7	1
Boone	Private	Forest edge	82,000	21	5	16	15	14	7	1
			425,000	126	74	52	49	41	18	3
Callaway	Private	Nonforest	179,000	45	41	4	4	2	0	0
Callaway	Private	Nonforest edge	114,000	37	17	20	17	11	2	3
Callaway	Private	Forest	126,000	33	2	31	28	28	16	3
Callaway	Private	Forest edge	97,000	34	7	27	26	21	11	1
			516,000	149	67	82	75	62	29	7
Cape Girardeau	Private	Nonforest	182,000	50	49	1	1	0	0	0
Cape Girardeau	Private	Nonforest edge	82,000	33	21	12	11	7	2	1
Cape Girardeau	Private	Forest	47,000	16	0	16	14	14	7	2
Cape Girardeau	Private	Forest edge	58,000	15	3	12	11	10	4	1
			369,000	114	73	41	37	31	13	4
Cole	Private	Nonforest	78,000	20	18	2	1	1	0	1
Cole	Private	Nonforest edge	73,000	22	16	6	6	4	2	0
Cole	Private	Forest	40,000	13	0	13	11	11	6	2
Cole	Private	Forest edge	61,000	20	3	17	15	14	8	2
			252,000	75	37	38	33	30	16	5
Franklin	Private	Nonforest	119,000	37	35	2	2	1	0	0
Franklin	Private	Nonforest edge	154,000	51	23	28	25	16	3	3
Franklin	Private	Forest	155,000	47	3	44	37	37	18	7
Franklin	Private	Forest edge	150,000	41	10	31	26	23	9	5
			578,000	176	71	105	90	77	30	15
Gasconade	Private	Nonforest	53,000	13	12	1	1	0	0	0
Gasconade	Private	Nonforest edge	76,000	29	12	17	15	10	2	2
Gasconade	Private	Forest	122,000	34	1	33	31	31	12	2
Gasconade	Private	Forest edge	83,000	22	2	20	16	14	5	4
			334,000	98	27	71	63	55	19	8

Table A.—continued

Unit- County[a]	Ownership layer[b]	Classified NLCD layer[c]	Area (Acres)[d]	Selected[e]	Nonforest office plots[f]	Field check plots[g]	Field check plots measured[h]	Forest plots measured[i]	Forest plots measured for change[j]	Plots not measured[k]
								Number of plots		
- Private Lands- Unit 5 (continued) -										
Howard	Private	Nonforest	129,000	37	36	1	1	0	0	0
Howard	Private	Nonforest edge	77,000	30	14	16	13	12	1	3
Howard	Private	Forest	31,000	8	0	8	7	7	3	1
Howard	Private	Forest edge	54,000	14	3	11	10	8	4	1
			291,000	89	53	36	31	27	8	5
Jefferson	Private	Nonforest	53,000	14	11	3	3	1	0	0
Jefferson	Private	Nonforest edge	91,000	25	13	12	9	8	2	3
Jefferson	Private	Forest	171,000	55	4	51	46	45	20	5
Jefferson	Private	Forest edge	107,000	34	6	28	28	25	6	0
			422,000	128	34	94	86	79	28	8
Mississippi,	Private	Nonforest	861,000	266	260	6	5	2	1	1
Scott, Stoddard	Private	Nonforest edge	101,000	29	19	10	9	6	1	1
Mississippi,	Private	Forest	26,000	11	0	11	10	9	3	1
Scott, Stoddard	Private	Forest edge	59,000	18	4	14	14	13	3	0
			1,047,000	324	283	41	38	30	8	3
Moniteau	Private	Nonforest	131,000	40	36	4	4	1	0	0
Moniteau	Private	Nonforest edge	65,000	21	12	9	9	6	2	0
Moniteau	Private	Forest	23,000	6	0	6	5	4	2	1
Moniteau	Private	Forest edge	44,000	11	2	9	7	7	4	2
			263,000	78	50	28	25	18	8	3
Montgomery	Private	Nonforest	152,000	40	40	0	0	0	0	0
Montgomery	Private	Nonforest edge	70,000	25	18	7	6	3	1	1
Montgomery	Private	Forest	68,000	19	1	18	16	16	6	2
Montgomery	Private	Forest edge	53,000	17	5	12	10	9	3	2
			343,000	101	64	37	32	28	10	5
Osage	Private	Nonforest	74,000	24	20	4	4	1	0	0
Osage	Private	Nonforest edge	102,000	31	15	16	14	9	2	2
Osage	Private	Forest	104,000	29	2	27	26	26	11	1
Osage	Private	Forest edge	105,000	32	1	31	26	23	10	5
			385,000	116	38	78	70	59	23	8
Pemiscot,	Private	Nonforest	1,008,000	311	305	6	6	1	0	0
Dunklin,	Private	Nonforest edge	55,000	20	13	7	6	2	0	1
New Madrid	Private	Forest	18,000	6	0	6	6	4	0	0
	Private	Forest edge	28,000	7	5	2	1	1	0	1
			1,109,000	344	323	21	19	8	0	2
Perry	Private	Nonforest	120,000	41	40	1	1	0	0	0
Perry	Private	Nonforest edge	71,000	18	10	8	5	4	0	3
Perry	Private	Forest	60,000	15	0	15	15	15	7	0
Perry	Private	Forest edge	58,000	19	5	14	14	14	3	0
			309,000	93	55	38	35	33	10	3
St. Charles	Private	Nonforest	191,000	55	53	2	2	1	1	0
St. Charles	Private	Nonforest edge	74,000	27	20	7	6	5	1	1
St. Charles	Private	Forest	37,000	10	0	10	9	9	4	1
St. Charles	Private	Forest edge	54,000	17	3	14	11	9	4	3
			356,000	109	76	33	28	24	10	5
Ste. Genevieve	Private	Nonforest	66,000	20	19	1	1	1	0	0
Ste. Genevieve	Private	Nonforest edge	61,000	22	8	14	13	11		1
Ste. Genevieve	Private	Forest	121,000	32	0	32	30	30	11	2
Ste. Genevieve	Private	Forest edge	62,000	23	4	19	15	15	4	4
			310,000	97	31	66	59	57	15	7
St. Louis, City	Private	Nonforest	246,000	83	79	4	4	1	1	0
of St. Louis	Private	Nonforest edge	57,000	12	7	5	4	3	0	1
St. Louis, City	Private	Forest	26,000	8	1	7	7	6	2	0
of St. Louis	Private	Forest edge	36,000	13	4	9	9	7	2	0
			365,000	116	91	25	24	17	5	1
Warren	Private	Nonforest	72,000	20	19	1	1	1	0	0
Warren	Private	Nonforest edge	53,000	9	5	4	4	1		0
Warren	Private	Forest	96,000	30	0	30	29	29	13	1
Warren	Private	Forest edge	52,000	20	1	19	19	17	6	0
			273,000	79	25	54	53	48	19	1
Unit 5 all co.		Total	7,947,000	2,412	1,472	940	847	724	269	93
All units	Private	All	41,783,000	8,745	4,802	3,943	3,607	3,092	1,734	336
- State total, all owners -										
All units	All owners	All	44,611,000	9,486	4,876	4,610	4,268	3,742	1,989	342

Table A.—continued

a Unit –County, the following table lists the counties in each county group used to define the estimation strata in Unit 4.

4A	4B	4NC	4NE	4NW	4RIV
Barton	Bates	Adair	Audrain	Caldwell	Andrew
Dade	Cass	Chariton	Clark	Clinton	Atchison
Greene	Cooper	Linn	Knox	Daviess	Buchanan
Jasper	Henry	Macon	Lewis	DeKalb	Carroll
Lawrence	Johnson	Putnam	Lincoln	Gentry	Clay
Vernon	Pettis	Randolph	Marion	Grundy	Holt
		Schuyler	Monroe	Harrison	Jackson
		Sullivan	Pike	Livingston	Lafayette
			Ralls	Mercer	Platte
			Scotland	Nodaway	Ray
			She by	Worth	Saline

bOwnership layer – Classification based on PAD.
cClassified NLCD layer – Classification based on the 1992 NLCD classification and 2-pixel edge zones.
dArea (Acres) – Total area defined by intersection of ownership and classified NLCD layers within group of counties specified.
eSelected – Total number of plots selected to be sampled.
fNonforest office plots – Selected plots whose observed classification as nonforest based on examination of aerial photographs and/or digital orthoquads.
gField check plots – Selected plots that required field measurement.
hField check plots measured– Field check plots where measurement was completed successfully. Excludes plots that were denied access, hazardous, or lost and measurement was not possible.
iForest plots measured – Field check plots where forest condition was present on plot and measurement was completed in 1999-2003 inventory. These plots are used to estimate current conditions, e.g., area, volume, number of trees and biomass.
jForest plots measured for change– Field check plots measured in both 1989 inventory and 1999-2003 inventory where a forest condition was found to on plot and measurement was completed. These plots are used to estimate change between inventories e.g., growth, removals, mortality, and area change.
kPlots not measured – Plots selected for field measurement but not measured due to denied access, hazardous condition, or other complications.

Table B.—State-level estimates of major forest resource attributes and their sampling errors

Item	State total	Sampling error
Growing Stock	(*Million cubic feet*)	(*Percent*)
Volume	14,638.2	1.39
Average annual net growth	629.4	2.61
Average annual removals	118.6	6.95
Average annual mortality	81.8	6.62
Sawtimber	(*Million board feet*)	
Volume	46,470.8	1.78
Average annual net growth	2,315.5	2.91
Average annual removals	454.0	7.46
Average annual mortality	212.2	1.17
Area	(*Thousand acres*)	
Forest land	14,576.5	0.80
Timberland	14,084.2	0.88

Table C.—Percent compliance to measurement quality objectives (MQO) tolerances of variables for blind check plots measured over 1999-2003

Variable	Measurement quality objective		Missouri		All Midwestern States	
	Tolerance	Objective	Percentage of data within tolerance	Number of observations	Percentage of data within tolerance	Number of observations
Tree Level						
Diameter at breast height	± 0.1 /20 inch	95.0	89.9	1,853	92.9	22,341
Diameter at root collar	± 0.1 /20 inch	95.0	0.0	0	60.7	28
Azimuth	± 10 °	90.0	98.8	1,853	98.4	22,369
Horizontal distance	± 0.2 /1.0 ft	90.0	96.4	1,853	97.1	22,369
Species	No tolerance	95.0	94.5	1,853	96.2	22,369
Tree genus	No tolerance	99.0	99.5	1,853	99.1	22,360
Tree status	No tolerance	95.0	98.4	1,853	99.1	22,369
Rotten/missing cull	± 10 percent	90.0	98.7	1,312	98.6	15,312
Total length	± 10 percent	90.0	75.1	1,221	82.4	14,424
Actual length	± 10 percent	90.0	63.9	83	80.1	1,638
Compacted crown ratio	± 10 percent	90.0	87.5	1,704	87.8	20,074
Uncompacted crown ratio	± 10 percent	90.0	59.2	76	78.2	724
Crown class	No tolerance	85.0	76.5	1,704	83.1	20,074
Decay class	± 1 class	90.0	100.0	131	100.0	2,048
Cause of death	No tolerance	80.0	86.3	131	93.6	2,048
Condition	No tolerance	99.0	98.1	1,853	97.4	22,369
Crown position	No tolerance	85.0	65.4	52	80.9	593
Crown light exposure	± 1 class	85.0	93.4	76	90.6	724
Sapling crown vigor class	No tolerance	85.0	54.2	24	61.4	132
Crown density	± 10 percent	90.0	50.0	52	67.6	593
Crown dieback	± 10 percent	90.0	96.2	52	96.5	593
Transparency	± 10 percent	90.0	71.2	52	84.0	593
NC tree class	No tolerance	90.0	88.5	1,830	92.3	22,054
NC damage agent 1	No tolerance	90.0	90.3	1,704	91.9	20,074
NC damage agent 2	No tolerance	90.0	89.3	272	87.0	3,235
Missouri damage code	No tolerance	90.0	69.9	1,483	69.9	1,483
Utilization	No tolerance	99.0	69.2	26	88.0	309
NC tree grade	No tolerance	90.0	54.3	328	68.5	3,566
D.b.h. of live and sound dead trees	± 0.1 /20 inch	95.0	89.9	1,724	92.6	20,505
D.b.h. of dead rotten trees	± 1 /20 inch	95.0	97.6	41	98.4	942
Total length trees 40 ft plus	± 10 percent	90.0	75.3	891	83.8	11,863
Total length trees < 40 ft	± 10 percent	90.0	74.5	330	75.8	2,561
Total length trees < 5 inches d.b.h.	± 10 percent	90.0	47.4	19	70.7	147
Seedling Level						
Species	No tolerance	85.0	85.2	629	91.2	4,680
Genus	No tolerance	90.0	96.0	629	97.2	4,680
Seedling count	± 20 percent	90.0	55.5	629	66.5	4,680
Seedling count coded	No tolerance	90.0	61.5	629	73.2	4,680

Table C.—continued

Variable	Measurement quality objective		Missouri		All Midwestern States	
	Tolerance	Objective	Percentage of data within tolerance	Number of observations	Percentage of data within tolerance	Number of observations
Condition Level						
Condition status	No tolerance	99.0	98.6	139	99.0	1,882
Reserve status	No tolerance	99.0	100.0	139	99.5	1,882
Owner group	No tolerance	99.0	98.1	104	98.3	1,487
Forest type (type)	No tolerance	95.0	79.8	104	80.3	1,487
Forest type (group)	No tolerance	99.0	91.3	104	89.4	1,487
Stand size	No tolerance	99.0	83.7	104	88.0	1,487
Regeneration status	No tolerance	99.0	99.0	104	99.1	1,487
Tree density	No tolerance	99.0	97.1	104	93.8	1,487
Owner class	No tolerance	99.0	93.3	104	95.4	1,487
Owner status	No tolerance	99.0	96.2	104	98.9	1,487
Regeneration species	No tolerance	99.0	99.0	104	98.9	1,487
Stand age	± 10 yrs	95.0	48.1	104	64.4	1,487
Disturbance 1	No tolerance	99.0	94.1	102	92.9	1,475
Disturbance year 1	± 1 yr	99.0	93.8	16	86.2	58
Disturbance 2	No tolerance	99.0	95.0	20	95.4	153
Disturbance year 2	± 1 yr	99.0	100.0	1	50.0	4
Disturbance 3	No tolerance	99.0	100.0	2	90.0	10
Disturbance year 3	± 1 yr	99.0	0.0	0	0.0	0
Treatment 1	No tolerance	99.0	92.2	102	95.0	1,475
Treatment year 1	± 1 yr	99.0	25.0	4	91.0	89
Treatment 2	No tolerance	99.0	100.0	12	85.8	162
Treatment year 2	± 1 yr	99.0	0.0	0	100.0	13
Treatment 3	No tolerance	99.0	0.0	0	97.1	35
Treatment year 3	± 1 yr	99.0	0.0	0	100.0	5
Physiographic class	No tolerance	80.0	70.2	104	75.4	1,487
Present nonforest use	No tolerance	90.0	100.0	35	99.8	629
NC land use	No tolerance	99.0	89.2	139	93.0	1,882
Subplot Level						
Subplot center condition	No tolerance	99.0	97.9	436	97.1	5,183
Microplot center condition	No tolerance	99.0	97.2	436	96.8	5,183
Slope	± 10 percent	90.0	95.6	436	97.5	5,183
Aspect	± 10 °	90.0	69.8	381	88.3	4,789
Snow/water depth	± 0.5 ft		94.3	436	66.2	5,183
Plot Level						
Distance to road	No tolerance	90.0	76.1	109	80.8	1,311
Water on plot	No tolerance	90.0	88.1	109	87.7	1,311
Road type code	No tolerance	90.0	64.0	100	76.0	1,028
Recreational use restrictions	No tolerance	90.0	85.0	100	90.4	1,028
Recreational use 1	No tolerance	90.0	96.0	100	94.3	1,028
Recreational use 2	No tolerance	90.0	0.0	0	100.0	16
Recreational use 3	No tolerance	90.0	0.0	0	90.9	11
Road access	No tolerance	90.0	83.5	109	93.5	1,311
Elevation	± 50 ft	99.0	78.2	101	81.5	1,177
Latitude (decimal degrees)	± 0.0001 dg	99.0	92.1	101	91.2	1,187
Longitude (decimal degrees)	± 0.0001 dg	99.0	88.1	101	90.6	1,187
Latitude (ft)	± 140 ft	99.0	99.0	101	98.1	1,187
Longitude (ft)	± 140 ft	99.0	98.0	101	97.6	1,187

Table C.—continued

Variable	Measurement quality objective		Missouri		All Midwestern States	
	Tolerance	Objective	Percentage of data within tolerance	Number of observations	Percentage of data within tolerance	Number of observations
Boundary Level						
Boundary change	No tolerance	99.0	94.7	19	95.3	275
Contrasting condition	No tolerance	99.0	100.0	19	92.4	275
Left azimuth	± 10 degrees	90.0	100.0	19	85.1	275
Corner mapped	No tolerance	90.0	94.7	19	97.5	275
Corner azimuth	± 10 degrees	90.0	100.0	2	60.0	10
Corner distance	± 1 ft	90.0	100.0	2	50.0	10
Right azimuth	± 10 degrees	90.0	89.5	19	84.7	275
Site Index Tree						
Condition list	No tolerance	99.0	95.0	160	90.6	2,652
Diameter	± 0.1 /20 in.	95.0	76.6	94	90.6	2,044
Species	No tolerance	95.0	93.1	160	95.7	2,652
Genus	No tolerance	99.0	99.4	160	99.7	2,652
Azimuth	± 10 degrees	90.0	93.6	94	98.1	2,044
Distance	± 5 feet	90.0	96.8	94	99.6	2,044
Total length	± 10 percent	90.0	83.0	94	90.5	2,044
Diameter age	± 5 years	95.0	62.8	94	78.1	2,044
Site index method	No tolerance	99.0	100.0	160	99.9	2,652
Field site index	No tolerance	99.0	78.1	160	93.3	2,652

Table D.—Observed relative bias values (average [field crew - QA crew]) for blind check plots measured over 1999-2003

Variable	Unit of measure	Missouri Rel. bias	95 % Conf. Int. lower limit	95 % Conf. Int. upper limit	No. of obs.	All Midwestern States Rel. bias	95 % Conf. Int. lower limit	95 % Conf. Int. upper limit	No. of obs.
Tree Level									
Diameter at breast height	inches	0.04	0.01	0.09	1,853	-0.02	-0.03	-0.01	22,341
Diameter at root collar	inches	0.00	0.00	0.00	.	0.11	-0.12	0.46	28
Azimuth	degrees	-0.50	-0.77	-0.21	1,853	0.31	0.19	0.41	22,369
Horizontal distance	feet	-0.01	-0.04	0.02	1,853	0.00	-0.01	0.01	22,369
Species	code	-1.36	-2.62	-0.37	1,853	0.01	-0.48	0.40	22,369
Tree genus	code	-1.29	-2.49	-0.26	1,853	0.01	-0.47	0.37	22,360
Tree status	code	0.01	0.00	0.02	1,853	0.00	0.00	0.00	22,369
Rotten/missing cull	%	-0.08	-0.28	0.13	1,312	0.01	-0.07	0.08	15,312
Total length	feet	-0.35	-1.10	0.35	1,221	0.24	-0.06	0.47	14,424
Actual length	feet	-5.3	-14.2	1.7	83	-1.9	-3.7	-0.6	1,638
Compacted crown ratio	%	0.86	0.45	1.36	1,704	0.48	0.34	0.61	20,074
Uncompacted crown ratio	%	-14.6	-20.2	-8.9	76	-6.6	-8.1	-5.1	724
Crown class	code	0.01	-0.02	0.04	1,704	0.02	0.01	0.03	20,074
Decay class	code	0.02	-0.12	0.19	131	0.06	0.03	0.03	2,048
Cause of death	code	3.66	0.69	6.68	131	1.56	1.04	1.04	2,048
Condition	code	0.01	0.01	0.02	1,853	0.00	0.00	0.01	22,369
Crown position	code	-0.52	-0.81	-0.25	52	-0.25	-0.31	-0.18	593
Crown light exposure	code	-0.24	-0.39	-0.08	76	-0.25	-0.31	-0.19	724
Sapling crown vigor class	code	-0.25	-0.50	0.04	24	-0.27	-0.37	-0.15	132
Crown density	%	-15.2	-21.0	-9.7	52	-7.1	-8.7	-5.4	593
Crown dieback	%	-1.63	-2.88	-0.58	52	-0.65	-1.41	-0.12	593
Transparency	%	-2.88	-5.77	-0.10	52	-3.53	-4.69	-2.35	593
NC tree class	code	0.40	0.21	0.60	1,830	0.11	0.07	0.16	22,054
NC damage agent 1	code	4.53	-0.17	8.63	1,704	5.17	3.83	6.54	20,074
NC damage agent 2	code	9.23	-5.33	23.00	272	5.4	0.9	9.9	3,235
Missouri damage code	code	67.92	48.25	90.93	1,483	67.92	47.16	47.16	1,483
Utilization	code	0.23	0.04	0.42	26	-0.02	-0.06	0.02	309
NC tree grade	code	-1.8	-15.1	13.3	328	-1.0	-4.5	2.5	3,566
D.b.h. of live and sound dead trees	inches	0.01	-0.02	0.04	1,724	-0.02	-0.03	-0.02	20,505
D.b.h. of dead rotten trees	inches	-0.07	-0.16	0.02	41	-0.04	-0.07	-0.01	942
Total length trees 40 ft plus	feet	0.27	-0.34	0.94	891	0.88	0.73	1.02	11,863
Total length trees < 40 ft	feet	-2.00	-3.66	-0.63	330	-2.70	-3.94	-1.61	2,561
Total length trees < 5 inches d.b.h.	feet	2.97	-5.68	11.40	19	2.30	-0.15	4.55	147
Seedling Level									
Species	code	0.00	-0.03	0.03	629	0.00	-0.01	0.01	4,680
Genus	code	0.01	-0.01	0.02	629	0.00	0.00	0.01	4,680
Seedling count	percent	-18.1	-23.8	-13.0	629	-11.3	-14.4	-8.6	4,680
Seedling count coded	percent	-0.05	-0.13	0.04	629	0.0	0.0	0.1	4,680

Table D.—continued

Variable	Unit of measure	Missouri Rel. bias	Missouri 95 % Conf. Int. lower limit	Missouri 95 % Conf. Int. upper limit	Missouri No. of obs.	All Midwestern States Rel. bias	All Midwestern States 95 % Conf. Int. lower limit	All Midwestern States 95 % Conf. Int. upper limit	No. of obs.
Condition Level									
Condition status	code	-0.09	-0.22	0.00	139	0.00	-0.02	0.01	1,882
Reserve status	code	0.00	0.00	0.00	139	0.00	0.00	0.01	1,882
Owner group	code	0.67	0.00	1.73	104	-0.05	-0.21	0.11	1,487
Forest type (type)	code	15.18	2.01	31.26	104	13.83	7.40	19.41	1,487
Forest type (group)	code	14.42	1.44	30.29	104	13.79	7.23	19.50	1,487
Stand size	code	0.12	0.02	0.22	104	-0.01	-0.03	0.02	1,487
Regeneration status	code	0.01	0.00	0.03	104	0.00	0.00	0.00	1,487
Tree density	code	0.03	0.00	0.07	104	0.00	-0.01	0.01	1,487
Owner class	code	0.68	-0.09	1.82	104	-0.06	-0.24	0.12	1,487
Owner status	code	-0.02	-0.06	0.01	104	0.00	-0.01	0.02	1,487
Regeneration species	code	1.06	0.00	3.17	104	0.03	-0.52	0.53	1,487
Stand age	years	-0.56	-3.02	2.52	104	-0.99	-1.75	-0.22	1,487
Disturbance 1	code	-0.81	-3.10	1.52	102	-1.64	-2.47	-0.97	1,475
Disturbance year 1	year	500	0	1499	16	1103	552	1793	58
Disturbance 2	code	-1.00	-3.50	0.00	20	-1.01	-2.48	0.25	153
Disturbance year 2	year	0	0	0	1	2000	0	5998	4
Disturbance 3	code	0.00	0.00	0.00	2	-8.00	-24.00	0.00	10
Disturbance year 3	year	0.00	0.00	0.00	0	0.00	0.00	0.00	0
Treatment 1	code	0.59	-0.25	1.67	102	0.15	-0.03	0.32	1,475
Treatment year 1	year	0.75	-1.50	3.00	4	0.13	-0.04	0.33	89
Treatment 2	code	0.00	0.00	0.00	12	4.07	2.01	6.14	162
Treatment year 2	year	0.00	0.00	0.00	0	0.08	-0.23	0.35	13
Treatment 3	code	0.00	0.00	0.00	0	-1.14	-3.43	0.00	35
Treatment year 3	year	0.00	0.00	0.00	0	0.00	0.00	0.00	5
Physiographic class	code	-0.80	-1.68	-0.08	104	0.02	-0.21	0.27	1,487
Present nonforest use	code	0.00	0.00	0.00	35	0.06	0.00	0.25	629
NC land use	code	-0.27	-2.22	1.90	139	0.04	-0.29	0.34	1,882
Subplot Level									
Subplot center condition	code	0.01	-0.01	0.02	436	0.00	0.00	0.01	5,183
Microplot center condition	code	0.01	0.00	0.03	436	0.01	0.00	0.01	5,183
Slope	%	0.49	-0.05	1.06	436	0.70	-0.60	1.86	5,183
Aspect	degrees	-5.5	-13.2	1.6	381	0.1	-1.5	1.8	4,789
Snow/water depth	feet	-0.08	-0.15	-0.01	436	-0.47	-0.90	-0.11	5,183
Plot Level									
Distance to oad	code	0.15	-0.02	0.33	109	0.00	-0.04	0.05	1,311
Water on plot	code	0.06	-0.26	0.35	109	0.13	0.01	0.24	1,311
Road type code	code	0.31	0.11	0.54	100	0.07	0.01	0.13	1,028
Recreational use restrictions	code	-0.42	-1.18	0.21	100	0.14	-0.11	0.39	1,028
Recreational use 1	code	-0.16	-0.36	0.00	100	-0.09	-0.15	-0.04	1,028
Recreational use 2	code	0.00	0.00	0.00	.	0.00	0.00	0.00	16
Recreational use 3	code	0.00	0.00	0.00	.	-0.09	-0.36	0.00	11
Road access	code	-0.06	-0.15	0.03	109	-0.04	-0.07	-0.02	1,311
Elevation	feet	-19.7	-39.7	-2.9	101	-35.9	-71.2	-7.3	1,177
Latitude	degrees	-0.03	-0.09	0.00	101	-0.01	-0.02	0.00	1,187
Longitude	degrees	8.33	0.00	25.00	101	0.71	0.00	2.84	1,187
Latitude	1,000 feet	-10.8	-32.5	.04	101	-2717	-6421	-106	1,187
Longitude	1,000 feet	110.0	-.02	319.2	101	11545	189	33863	1,187

37

Table D.—continued

Variable	Unit of measure	Missouri Rel. bias	Missouri 95 % Conf. Int. lower limit	Missouri 95 % Conf. Int. upper limit	No. of obs.	All Midwestern States Rel. bias	All Midwestern States 95 % Conf. Int. lower limit	All Midwestern States 95 % Conf. Int. upper limit	No. of obs.
Boundary Level									
Boundary change	code	0.11	0.00	0.32	19	0.08	0.03	0.13	275
Contrasting condition	code	0.00	0.00	0.00	19	0.00	-0.03	0.03	275
Left azimuth	degrees	1.47	-0.21	3.05	19	-4.67	-9.80	-0.02	275
Corner mapped	code	0.05	0.00	0.16	19	-0.01	-0.03	0.01	275
Corner azimuth	degrees	3.5	-12.0	19.0	0	1.6	-4.8	9.1	10
Corner distance	feet	0.50	0.00	1.00	2	-1.60	-8.60	2.80	10
Right azimuth	degrees	-3.74	-8.87	-0.24	19	2.00	-2.79	7.52	275
Site Index Tree									
Condition list	code	0.35	0.01	0.76	160	0.21	-0.10	0.44	2,652
Diameter	inches	0.02	-0.04	0.11	94	-0.01	-0.03	0.01	2,044
Species	code	-0.54	-1.69	0.30	160	-0.04	-0.24	0.17	2,652
Genus	code	-0.33	-0.99	0.00	160	-0.03	-0.22	0.17	2,652
Azimuth	degrees	-0.79	-6.41	4.92	94	-0.11	-0.58	0.40	2,044
Distance	feet	0.24	-0.32	0.75	94	0.05	0.02	0.10	2,044
Total length	feet	-0.84	-2.34	0.79	94	0.26	-0.09	0.60	2,044
Diameter age	years	-3.46	-6.02	-1.36	94	0.20	-0.08	0.49	2,044
Site-index method	code	0.00	0.00	0.00	160	0.00	0.00	0.00	2,652
Field site index	feet	0.53	0.18	0.95	160	0.48	0.26	0.69	2,652

Table E.—FIA nonresponse by strata for annual inventories measured in 1999-2003

Owner-Strata	Number of plots selected	Observed	Denied access	Hazardous	Other	Percent response rate
			Sum of plot portions[a]			
			Missouri			
National Forest						
Nonforest	1	1.0	0.0	0.0	0.0	100.0
Nonforest edge	9	9.0	0.0	0.0	0.0	100.0
Forest edge	8	8.0	0.0	0.0	0.0	100.0
Forest	410	408.0	2.0	0.0	0.0	99.5
Total	428	426.0	2.0	0.0	0.0	99.5
Other Public						
Nonforest	47	47.0	0.0	0.0	0.0	100.0
Nonforest edge	35	35.0	0.0	0.0	0.0	100.0
Forest edge	44	42.8	1.0	0.3	0.0	97.2
Forest	187	184.0	3.0	0.0	0.0	98.4
Total	313	308.8	4.0	0.3	0.0	98.6
Private						
Nonforest	3,674	3,665.8	7.0	0.3	1.0	99.8
Nonforest edge	1,742	1,671.7	69.3	1.1	0.0	96.0
Forest edge	1,400	1,308.5	90.3	1.3	0.0	93.5
Forest	1,929	1,758.2	163.9	5.9	1.0	91.1
Total	8,745	8,404.1	330.4	8.5	2.0	96.1
Total	9,486	9,138.9	336.4	8.7	2.0	96.3
			All Midwestern States			
National Forest						
Nonforest	125	125.0	0.0	0.0	0.0	100.0
Nonforest edge	156	156.0	0.0	0.0	0.0	100.0
Forest edge	314	311.0	0.0	3.0	0.0	99.0
Forest	2,547	2,516.5	3.3	24.3	3.0	98.8
Total	3,142	3,108.5	3.3	27.3	3.0	98.9
Other Public						
Nonforest	1,037	1,035.0	1.0	1.0	0.0	99.8
Nonforest edge	664	658.0	2.0	3.0	1.0	99.1
Forest edge	946	932.8	3.0	8.3	2.0	98.6
Forest	3,837	3,762.8	9.0	29.3	36.0	98.1
Total	6,484	6,388.5	15.0	41.5	39.0	98.5
Private						
Nonforest	47,137	47,032.5	98.0	1.5	5.0	99.8
Nonforest edge	10,272	9,916.8	335.1	10.2	10.0	96.5
Forest edge	8,011	7,464.2	527.4	11.4	8.0	93.2
Forest	10,327	9,664.5	624.1	19.4	19.0	93.6
Total	75,747	74,077.9	1,584.6	42.5	42.0	97.8
Total	85,373	83,574.9	1,602.8	111.3	84.0	97.9

[a] Indicates the total sum of the plot area in a category. For example a value of 2.0 denied access could indicate that 2 entire plots were denied access or 1 entire plot and two subplots on two other plots were denied access.

Table 1. -- Percentage of area by land status, Missouri, 1999-2003

Land status	Percentage of area
Accessible forest land	
Unreserved forest land	
Timberland	29.6
Unproductive	0.5
Total unreserved forest land	30.1
Reserved forest land	
Productive	0.6
Unproductive	- -
Total reserved forest land	0.6
All accessible forest land	30.7
Nonforest and other land	
Water	64.2
Nonforest land	
Census	1.1
Non-Census	0.7
All nonforest and other land	66.0
Nonsampled land	
Access denied	3.2
Hazardous conditions	0.1
Other	- -
All land	100.0
Total area (thousands of acres)	44,611

All table cells without observations in the inventory sample are indicated
by --. Table value of 0.0 indicates the percentage rounds to less than 0.1
percent. Columns and rows may not add to their totals due to rounding.

40

Table 2. -- Area of forest land, in thousand acres, by owner class and forest-land status, Missouri, 1999-2003

Owner class	Unreserved forests			Reserved forests			All forest land
	Timberland	Unproductive	Total	Productive	Unproductive	Total	
Forest Service							
National forest	1,379.8	12.1	1,392.0	76.8	- -	76.8	1,468.8
Other Federal							
National Park Service	- -	- -	- -	61.6	- -	61.6	61.6
Fish and Wildlife Service	12.2	- -	12.2	- -	- -	- -	12.2
Department of Defense or Energy	60.3	5.1	65.4	- -	- -	- -	65.4
Other Federal	164.5	6.2	170.7	32.4	- -	32.4	203.1
State and local government							
State	636.3	6.7	643.0	87.2	- -	87.2	730.2
Local (county, municipal, etc.)	63.4	- -	63.4	4.2	- -	4.2	67.5
Other non-Federal lands	1.1	- -	1.1	- -	- -	- -	1.1
Private							
Undifferentiated private	11,747.3	212.1	11,959.5	7.2	- -	7.2	11,966.7
All owners	14,064.9	242.3	14,307.1	269.3	- -	269.3	14,576.4

All table cells without observations in the inventory sample are indicated by --. Table value of 0.0 indicates the acres round to less than 0.1 thousand acres. Columns and rows may not add to their totals due to rounding.

41

Table 3. -- Area of forest land, in thousand acres, by forest-type group and productivity class, Missouri, 1999-2003

Forest type group	Site productivity class (cubic feet/acre/year)							All classes
	0-19	20-49	50-84	85-119	120-164	165-224	225+	
White / red / jack pine group	--	--	--	--	1.5	--	--	1.5
Loblolly / shortleaf pine group	0.4	11.8	34.1	98.0	16.8	--	--	161.1
Other eastern softwoods group	1.9	257.2	32.6	21.6	--	--	--	313.2
Exotic softwoods group	--	1.4	--	--	--	--	--	1.4
Oak / pine group	16.9	397.4	264.7	201.7	29.4	--	6.0	916.1
Oak / hickory group	218.9	3,258.0	5,860.6	2,463.2	188.2	14.9	5.0	12,008.8
Oak / gum / cypress group	--	7.1	27.8	23.5	4.0	7.0	--	69.4
Elm / ash / cottonwood group	3.2	269.2	350.5	272.5	6.2	3.0	--	904.7
Maple / beech / birch group	1.0	39.9	20.3	10.9	--	--	--	72.1
Other hardwoods group	--	18.9	9.0	--	--	--	--	27.9
Exotic hardwoods group	--	--	2.3	--	--	--	--	2.3
Nonstocked	--	42.3	41.9	9.5	4.1	--	--	97.8
All forest type groups	242.3	4,303.2	6,643.8	3,100.9	250.3	25.0	11.0	14,576.4

All table cells without observations in the inventory sample are indicated by --. Table value of 0.0 indicates the acres round to less than 0.1 thousand acres. Columns and rows may not add to their totals due to rounding.

Table 4. – Area of forest land, in thousand acres, by forest-type group, ownership group, and land status, Missouri, 1999-2003

Forest type group	Forest Service		Other Federal		State and local government		Undifferentiated private		All forest land
	Timber-land	Other forest land	Timber-land	Other forest land	Timber-land	Other forest land	Timber-land	Other forest land	
White / red / jack pine group	--	--	--	--	1.5	--	--	--	1.5
Loblolly / shortleaf pine group	85.2	3.9	--	0.9	2.5	3.1	65.4	--	161.1
Other eastern softwoods group	12.6	2.6	4.3	--	0.8	--	287.7	5.2	313.2
Exotic softwoods group	--	--	--	--	1.4	--	--	--	1.4
Oak / pine group	192.5	10.6	20.0	11.0	48.0	6.6	610.5	16.9	916.1
Oak / hickory group	1,083.4	71.8	156.9	76.6	575.9	72.0	9,779.3	193.0	12,008.8
Oak / gum / cypress group	--	--	14.0	3.1	3.2	--	49.1	--	69.4
Elm / ash / cottonwood group	2.8	--	35.4	6.7	58.0	16.5	782.1	3.2	904.7
Maple / beech / birch group	0.9	--	0.9	6.9	--	--	62.3	1.0	72.1
Other hardwoods group	--	--	--	--	2.5	--	25.4	--	27.9
Exotic hardwoods group	--	--	--	--	--	--	2.3	--	2.3
Nonstocked	2.3	--	--	--	6.9	--	83.1	--	97.8
All forest type groups	1,379.8	88.9	237.0	105.2	700.7	98.1	11,747.3	219.3	14,576.4

All table cells without observations in the inventory sample are indicated by --. Table value of 0.0 indicates the acres round to less than 0.1 thousand acres. Columns and rows may not add to their totals due to rounding.

Table 5. -- Area of forest land, in thousand acres, by forest-type group and stand-size class, Missouri, 1999-2003

Forest type group	Stand-size class					All size classes
	Large diameter	Medium diameter	Small diameter	Chaparral	Nonstocked	
White / red / jack pine group	1.5	--	--	--	--	1.5
Loblolly / shortleaf pine group	111.0	46.6	3.6	--	--	161.1
Other eastern softwoods group	52.1	124.0	137.0	--	--	313.2
Exotic softwoods group	1.4	--	--	--	--	1.4
Oak / pine group	374.0	413.0	129.1	--	--	916.1
Oak / hickory group	6,263.8	4,589.9	1,155.2	--	--	12,008.8
Oak / gum / cypress group	44.1	18.2	7.1	--	--	69.4
Elm / ash / cottonwood group	555.9	245.7	103.1	--	--	904.7
Maple / beech / birch group	35.8	29.6	6.7	--	--	72.1
Other hardwoods group	--	1.4	26.5	--	--	27.9
Exotic hardwoods group	2.3	--	--	--	--	2.3
Nonstocked	--	--	--	--	97.8	97.8
All forest type groups	7,441.9	5,468.5	1,568.2	--	97.8	14,576.4

All table cells without observations in the inventory sample are indicated by --. Table value of 0.0 indicates the acres round to less than 0.1 thousand acres. Columns and rows may not add to their totals due to rounding.

Table 6. – Area of forest land, in thousand acres, by forest-type group and stand-age class, Missouri, 1999-2003

Forest type group	Non stocked	Stand-age class (years)											All classes
		1-20	21-40	41-60	61-80	81-100	101-120	121-140	141-160	161-180	181-200	201+	
White / red / jack pine group	--	--	1.5	--	--	--	--	--	--	--	--	--	1.5
Loblolly / shortleaf pine group	--	11.6	44.3	76.2	17.9	11.1	--	--	--	--	--	--	161.1
Other eastern softwoods group	--	65.9	96.5	110.0	29.0	5.3	--	--	--	--	--	--	313.2
Exotic softwoods group	--	--	1.4	--	--	--	--	--	--	--	--	--	1.4
Oak / pine group	--	84.8	175.9	330.8	244.6	66.2	13.8	--	--	--	--	--	916.1
Oak / hickory group	--	911.7	1,798.5	4,160.9	3,328.9	1,304.5	329.1	130.9	15.9	--	4.2	7.8	12,008.8
Oak / gum / cypress group	--	7.1	29.8	19.8	12.7	--	--	--	--	--	--	--	69.4
Elm / ash / cottonwood group	--	127.0	229.0	377.5	147.3	14.1	8.9	--	--	--	--	--	904.7
Maple / beech / birch group	--	4.4	9.3	22.2	23.4	9.6	--	3.3	--	--	--	--	72.1
Other hardwoods group	--	26.5	1.4	--	--	--	--	--	--	--	--	--	27.9
Exotic hardwoods group	--	2.3	--	--	--	--	--	--	--	--	--	--	2.3
Nonstocked	97.8	--	--										97.8
All forest type groups	97.8	1,241.2	2,387.7	5,097.4	3,803.9	1,410.7	351.8	134.2	15.9	--	4.2	7.8	14,576.4

All table cells without observations in the inventory sample are indicated by --. Table value of 0.0 indicates the acres round to less than 0.1 thousand acres. Columns and rows may not add to their totals due to rounding.

45

Table 7. -- Area of forest land, in thousand acres, by forest-type group and stand origin, Missouri, 1999-2003

Forest type group	Stand origin		All forest land
	Natural stands	Artificial regeneration	
White / red / jack pine group	--	1.5	1.5
Loblolly / shortleaf pine group	131.4	29.7	161.1
Other eastern softwoods group	312.0	1.2	313.2
Exotic softwoods group	--	1.4	1.4
Oak / pine group	901.0	15.1	916.1
Oak / hickory group	12,001.4	7.4	12,008.8
Oak / gum / cypress group	69.4	--	69.4
Elm / ash / cottonwood group	902.7	2.0	904.7
Maple / beech / birch group	72.1	--	72.1
Other hardwoods group	27.9	--	27.9
Exotic hardwoods group	2.3	--	2.3
Nonstocked	97.8	--	97.8
All forest type groups	**14,518.0**	**58.4**	**14,576.4**

All table cells without observations in the inventory sample are indicated by --. Table value of 0.0 indicates the acres round to less than 0.1 thousand acres. Columns and rows may not add to their totals due to rounding.

46

Table 8. -- Area of forest land, in thousand acres, by forest-type group and primary disturbance class, Missouri, 1999-2003

Forest type group	None	Insects	Disease	Weather	Fire	Domestic animals	Wild animals	Human	Other	All forest land
White / red / jack pine group	1.5	--	--	--	--	--	--	--	--	1.5
Loblolly / shortleaf pine group	148.9	--	3.5	--	3.1	5.6	--	--	--	161.1
Other eastern softwoods group	247.2	--	--	--	6.1	48.0	--	7.7	4.2	313.2
Exotic softwoods group	1.4	--	--	--	--	--	--	--	--	1.4
Oak / pine group	760.3	--	--	26.5	9.8	90.0	2.1	25.0	2.4	916.1
Oak / hickory group	9,602.0	34.7	47.4	225.7	258.5	1,501.1	21.7	229.8	87.8	12,008.8
Oak / gum / cypress group	56.6	--	--	11.6	--	1.2	--	--	--	69.4
Elm / ash / cottonwood group	481.3	--	7.9	236.0	11.4	75.2	3.4	22.5	67.0	904.7
Maple / beech / birch group	70.2	--	--	--	--	1.9	--	--	--	72.1
Other hardwoods group	25.3	--	--	--	--	1.5	--	--	1.2	27.9
Exotic hardwoods group	2.3	--	--	--	--	--	--	--	--	2.3
Nonstocked	52.8	2.8	--	6.3	--	22.1	--	10.7	3.1	97.8
All forest type groups	**11,449.8**	**37.6**	**58.8**	**506.2**	**288.9**	**1,746.6**	**27.2**	**295.7**	**165.6**	**14,576.4**

All table cells without observations in the inventory sample are indicated by --. Table value of 0.0 indicates the acres round to less than 0.1 thousand acres. Columns and rows may not add to their totals due to rounding.

47

Table 9. – Area of timberland, in thousand acres, by forest-type group and stand-size class, Missouri, 1999-2003

Forest type group	Large diameter	Medium diameter	Small diameter	Chaparral	Nonstocked	All size classes
White / red / jack pine group	1.5	--	--		--	1.5
Loblolly / shortleaf pine group	103.4	46.2	3.6		--	153.2
Other eastern softwoods group	52.1	121.4	131.8		--	305.3
Exotic softwoods group	1.4	--	--		--	1.4
Oak / pine group	367.0	386.8	117.3		--	871.1
Oak / hickory group	6,044.6	4,440.4	1,110.6		--	11,595.5
Oak / gum / cypress group	41.0	18.2	7.1		--	66.3
Elm / ash / cottonwood group	536.9	238.3	103.1		--	878.3
Maple / beech / birch group	34.0	23.4	6.7		--	64.1
Other hardwoods group	--	1.4	26.5		--	27.9
Exotic hardwoods group	2.3	--	--		--	2.3
Nonstocked	--	--	--		97.8	97.8
All forest type groups	7,184.2	5,276.2	1,506.6	--	97.8	14,064.9

All table cells without observations in the inventory sample are indicated by --. Table value of 0.0 indicates the acres round to less than 0.1 thousand acres. Columns and rows may not add to their totals due to rounding.

Table 10. — Number of live trees, in thousands, on forest land by species group and diameter class, Missouri, 1999-2003

Species group	Diameter class (inches)															All classes
	1.0-2.9	3.0-4.9	5.0-6.9	7.0-8.9	9.0-10.9	11.0-12.9	13.0-14.9	15.0-16.9	17.0-18.9	19.0-20.9	21.0-24.9	25.0-28.9	29.0-32.9	33.0-36.9	37.0+	
Softwood species groups																
Eastern softwood species groups																
Loblolly and shortleaf pines	24,308	24,061	23,761	20,617	17,100	11,572	5,925	2,442	1,035	533	140	--	--	--	--	131,493
Other yellow pines	--	--	71	63	77	--	--	--	--	--	--	--	--	--	--	211
Eastern white and red pines	--	--	15	96	71	145	118	--	--	--	--	--	--	--	--	445
Cypress	--	--	--	--	--	24	--	--	--	--	--	--	--	--	--	24
Other eastern softwoods	367,154	168,567	77,392	35,128	14,457	5,503	2,507	669	197	65	25	24	--	--	--	671,688
All softwoods	391,462	192,627	101,239	55,905	31,704	17,245	8,550	3,112	1,231	598	165	24	--	--	--	803,862
Hardwood species groups																
Eastern hardwood species groups																
Select white oaks	320,614	190,716	116,586	81,956	61,254	45,362	31,334	19,424	10,577	5,503	4,232	1,202	336	238	61	889,394
Select red oaks	46,480	28,539	18,529	14,158	10,537	8,075	6,847	4,826	3,115	2,555	1,595	473	167	112	59	146,065
Other white oaks	191,898	109,836	82,802	65,891	41,176	24,332	14,244	8,428	4,240	1,896	1,282	262	135	55	--	546,477
Other red oaks	413,273	171,968	107,030	79,198	62,786	46,068	30,159	18,072	10,189	5,467	4,045	1,139	263	139	41	949,839
Hickory	649,056	210,821	98,005	57,864	31,340	19,022	9,138	4,680	1,913	882	724	182	41	--	--	1,083,647
Hard maple	158,236	45,488	16,570	7,479	4,689	2,456	930	769	505	416	116	50	--	--	--	237,704
Soft maple	111,326	16,626	7,266	4,802	3,066	2,261	1,483	1,407	522	701	566	478	130	105	37	150,777
Beech	191	--	27	15	15	--	43	18	18	--	15	--	--	--	15	361
Sweetgum	5,758	941	764	680	345	156	143	164	131	73	--	--	--	--	--	9,156
Tupelo and blackgum	150,394	31,968	8,483	3,191	1,487	830	649	255	198	159	94	--	--	--	--	197,708
Ash	165,565	41,848	19,147	11,892	7,667	4,260	2,663	1,961	696	421	172	126	--	--	--	256,436
Cottonwood and aspen	7,712	755	620	459	129	371	81	352	384	347	173	72	91	87	106	11,740
Basswood	2,539	770	663	601	476	361	192	100	107	88	134	--	--	--	--	6,030
Yellow-poplar	1,549	390	168	107	62	98	158	59	19	63	56	--	--	--	--	2,747
Black walnut	33,612	20,110	13,041	10,869	8,275	6,770	3,783	2,106	1,522	835	315	200	79	36	--	101,552
Other eastern soft hardwoods	949,786	273,356	99,824	48,966	23,767	13,671	7,190	4,020	2,452	1,284	1,086	460	140	196	--	1,426,216
Other eastern hard hardwoods	675,625	139,069	31,837	14,650	8,194	4,626	2,780	1,227	1,217	653	232	163	115	--	--	880,387
Eastern noncommercial hardwoods	380,676	64,404	18,963	6,876	3,234	1,439	875	386	95	36	136	47	--	--	--	477,067
All hardwoods	4,264,290	1,347,604	640,226	409,673	268,518	180,159	112,665	68,273	37,899	21,359	14,972	4,854	1,497	968	320	7,373,305
All species groups	4,655,752	1,540,231	741,464	465,578	300,222	197,403	121,245	71,384	39,131	21,957	15,137	4,877	1,497	968	320	8,177,167

All table cells without observations in the inventory sample are indicated by -- Table value of 0 indicates the number of trees rounds to less than 1 thousand trees. Columns and rows may not add to their totals due to rounding.

Table 11. -- Number of growing-stock trees, in thousands, on timberland by species group and diameter class, Missouri, 1999-2003

Species group	Diameter class (inches)													All classes
	5.0-6.9	7.0-8.9	9.0-10.9	11.0-12.9	13.0-14.9	15.0-16.9	17.0-18.9	19.0-20.9	21.0-24.9	25.0-28.9	29.0-32.9	33.0-36.9	37.0+	
Softwood species groups														
Eastern softwood species groups														
Loblolly and shortleaf pines	22,901	19,926	16,092	10,921	5,616	2,344	961	469	81	--	--	--	--	79,312
Other yellow pines	71	21	35	--	--	--	--	--	--	--	--	--	--	127
Eastern white and red pines	15	96	52	127	99	--	--	--	--	--	--	--	--	390
Cypress	--	--	--	24	--	--	--	--	--	--	--	--	--	24
Other eastern softwoods	64,926	27,871	11,147	3,709	1,904	419	93	47	25	24	--	--	--	110,165
All softwoods	87,913	47,915	27,327	14,781	7,620	2,763	1,054	517	107	24	--	--	--	190,019
Hardwood species groups														
Eastern hardwood species groups														
Select white oaks	100,243	72,075	53,273	39,164	26,303	16,117	8,040	4,053	2,874	638	157	148	--	323,085
Select red oaks	15,737	12,082	9,093	6,583	5,889	3,861	2,703	2,107	1,268	411	61	79	23	59,898
Other white oaks	69,580	55,886	33,546	18,412	10,386	5,611	2,180	1,053	421	69	92	55	--	197,292
Other red oaks	89,898	67,809	54,636	39,705	25,951	15,179	8,258	4,305	2,680	702	149	21	20	309,314
Hickory	85,794	50,195	27,367	16,536	7,462	4,005	1,622	613	465	120	--	--	--	194,178
Hard maple	13,747	6,188	3,955	1,747	803	518	283	253	58	--	--	--	--	27,553
Soft maple	4,870	3,020	1,874	1,115	844	1,078	286	384	311	219	--	105	--	14,104
Beech	--	15	15	--	25	--	--	--	--	--	--	--	--	56
Sweetgum	655	600	327	156	119	109	112	52	--	--	--	--	--	2,130
Tupelo and blackgum	7,391	2,830	1,351	647	512	216	116	81	76	--	--	--	--	13,219
Ash	13,486	7,902	5,318	2,916	1,824	1,521	526	331	146	34	--	--	--	34,005
Cottonwood and aspen	588	295	91	328	47	352	337	347	173	47	63	87	106	2,865
Basswood	433	482	339	265	86	100	47	88	120	--	--	--	--	1,960
Yellow-poplar	132	88	82	79	158	59	19	44	--	--	--	--	--	662
Black walnut	9,202	7,935	6,124	5,085	2,897	1,535	1,256	578	215	160	--	--	--	34,986
Other eastern soft hardwoods	67,085	32,162	16,256	9,435	4,839	2,933	1,898	1,027	691	362	106	85	--	136,879
Other eastern hard hardwoods	16,422	7,990	4,712	2,129	1,556	264	436	320	22	33	41	--	--	33,924
All hardwoods	495,264	327,554	218,362	144,303	89,701	53,457	28,118	15,637	9,521	2,795	668	580	149	1,386,109
All species groups	583,177	375,469	245,688	159,084	97,321	56,220	29,172	16,154	9,628	2,819	668	580	149	1,576,128

All table cells without observations in the inventory sample are indicated by --. Table value of 0 indicates the number of trees rounds to less than 1 thousand trees. Columns and rows may not add to their totals due to rounding.

Table 12. -- Net volume, in million cubic feet, of all live trees by owner class and forest land status, Missouri, 1999-2003

Owner class	Unreserved forests			Reserved forests			All forest land
	Timberland	Unproductive	Total	Productive	Unproductive	Total	
Forest Service							
National forest	1,912.0	6.3	1,918.3	109.2	- -	109.2	2,027.5
Other Federal							
National Park Service	- -	- -	- -	98.6	- -	98.6	98.6
Fish and Wildlife Service	30.2	- -	30.2	- -	- -	- -	30.2
Department of Defense or Energy	59.1	0.8	59.9	- -	- -	- -	59.9
Other Federal	190.3	2.1	192.4	33.5	- -	33.5	225.9
State and local government							
State	847.0	4.2	851.2	151.2	- -	151.2	1,002.3
Local (county, municipal, etc.)	73.7	- -	73.7	5.6	- -	5.6	79.3
Other non-Federal lands	2.3	- -	2.3	- -	- -	- -	2.3
Private							
Undifferentiated private	14,292.4	202.1	14,494.5	5.6	- -	5.6	14,500.1
All owners	17,406.9	215.5	17,622.4	403.7	- -	403.7	18,026.1

All table cells without observations in the inventory sample are indicated by --. Table value of 0.0 indicates the volume rounds to less than 0.1 million cubic feet. Columns and rows may not add to their totals due to rounding.

51

Table 13. -- Net volume, in million cubic feet, of all live trees on forest land by forest-type group and stand-size class, Missouri, 1999-2003

Forest type group	Stand-size class					All size classes
	Large diameter	Medium diameter	Small diameter	Chaparral	Nonstocked	
White / red / jack pine group	4.8	--	--	--	--	4.8
Loblolly / shortleaf pine group	231.7	73.7	0.9	--	--	306.3
Other eastern softwoods group	59.2	84.9	35.4	--	--	179.5
Exotic softwoods group	0.3	--	--	--	--	0.3
Oak / pine group	576.4	428.7	30.9	--	--	1,036.0
Oak / hickory group	9,968.9	4,527.4	289.7	--	--	14,786.0
Oak / gum / cypress group	81.6	14.0	1.1	--	--	96.7
Elm / ash / cottonwood group	1,271.6	222.9	18.2	--	--	1,512.7
Maple / beech / birch group	67.4	22.5	3.2	--	--	93.0
Other hardwoods group	--	0.9	2.0	--	--	2.9
Exotic hardwoods group	4.2	--	--	--	--	4.2
Nonstocked	--	--	--	--	3.7	3.7
All forest type groups	12,266.0	5,375.0	381.5	--	3.7	18,026.1

All table cells without observations in the inventory sample are indicated by --. Table value of 0.0 indicates the volume rounds to less than 0.1 million cubic feet. Columns and rows may not add to their totals due to rounding.

Table 14. -- Net volume, in million cubic feet, of all live trees on forest land by species group and ownership group, Missouri, 1999-2003

Species group	Forest Service	Other Federal	State and local government	Undifferentiated private	All owners
Softwood species groups					
Eastern softwood species groups					
Loblolly and shortleaf pines	392.3	15.9	69.9	328.7	806.9
Other yellow pines	--	--	0.5	0.5	1.0
Eastern white and red pines	--	--	3.8	2.3	6.1
Cypress	--	--	--	0.3	0.3
Other eastern softwoods	38.5	8.2	10.7	481.2	538.6
All softwoods	430.8	24.2	84.9	813.0	1,352.9
Hardwood species groups					
Eastern hardwood species groups					
Select white oaks	505.3	106.8	253.8	3,299.5	4,165.4
Select red oaks	109.4	37.1	67.4	853.4	1,067.4
Other white oaks	153.9	43.4	57.4	1,659.7	1,914.5
Other red oaks	591.3	69.5	247.8	3,143.3	4,051.9
Hickory	121.0	36.3	83.7	1,387.6	1,628.6
Hard maple	18.1	4.1	10.5	232.6	265.3
Soft maple	3.7	6.6	77.6	293.9	381.8
Beech	--	--	4.0	2.1	6.1
Sweetgum	0.3	4.2	1.5	21.8	27.9
Tupelo and blackgum	19.6	0.9	6.3	66.5	93.2
Ash	10.3	7.2	14.1	361.9	393.6
Cottonwood and aspen	--	4.9	26.1	123.2	154.2
Basswood	1.1	0.2	1.2	37.2	39.8
Yellow-poplar	--	--	10.5	10.6	21.1
Black walnut	16.2	11.1	38.9	443.3	509.5
Other eastern soft hardwoods	38.9	46.4	75.3	1,243.6	1,404.2
Other eastern hard hardwoods	5.3	10.0	19.1	381.7	416.0
Eastern noncommercial hardwoods	2.2	1.7	3.9	124.9	132.7
All hardwoods	1,596.7	390.5	998.9	13,687.1	16,673.2
All species groups	2,027.5	414.7	1,083.9	14,500.1	18,026.1

All table cells without observations in the inventory sample are indicated by --. Table value of 0.0 indicates the volume rounds to less than 0.1 million cubic feet. Columns and rows may not add to their totals due to rounding.

Table 15. -- Net volume, in million cubic feet, of all live trees on forest land by species group and diameter class, Missouri, 1999-2003

Species group	Diameter class (inches)													All classes
	5.0-6.9	7.0-8.9	9.0-10.9	11.0-12.9	13.0-14.9	15.0-16.9	17.0-18.9	19.0-20.9	21.0-24.9	25.0-28.9	29.0-32.9	33.0-36.9	37.0+	
Softwood species groups														
Eastern softwood species groups														
Loblolly and shortleaf pines	55	105	161	179	137	80	46	32	11	--	--	--	--	807
Other yellow pines	0	0	1	--	--	--	--	--	--	--	--	--	--	1
Eastern white and red pines	0	0	1	2	3	--	--	--	--	--	--	--	--	6
Cypress	--	--	--	0	--	--	--	--	--	--	--	--	--	0
Other eastern softwoods	152	146	106	64	44	16	6	3	2	2	--	--	--	539
All softwoods	207	252	268	245	183	96	52	34	13	2	--	--	--	1,353
Hardwood species groups														
Eastern hardwood species groups														
Select white oaks	260	395	532	631	642	555	402	269	281	113	39	38	9	4,165
Select red oaks	44	71	94	113	143	140	123	128	112	48	20	18	12	1,067
Other white oaks	174	290	323	305	265	217	140	83	71	20	17	9	--	1,914
Other red oaks	235	374	542	641	623	527	399	274	264	110	35	18	8	4,052
Hickory	208	279	284	288	206	155	86	48	51	20	5	--	--	1,629
Hard maple	39	39	45	38	21	25	22	23	9	5	--	--	--	265
Soft maple	17	24	28	33	33	46	21	38	41	51	18	21	12	382
Beech	0	0	0	--	1	1	1	--	1	--	--	--	3	6
Sweetgum	1	3	3	2	3	5	6	4	--	--	--	--	--	28
Tupelo and blackgum	15	13	12	11	13	8	7	7	7	--	--	--	--	93
Ash	38	54	62	59	53	59	28	21	11	9	--	--	--	394
Cottonwood and aspen	2	2	1	6	2	12	18	22	14	9	15	20	33	154
Basswood	2	3	4	5	4	3	4	5	10	--	--	--	--	40
Yellow-poplar	0	1	1	2	4	3	1	4	5	--	--	--	--	21
Black walnut	27	50	67	90	73	56	57	38	19	19	10	4	--	510
Other eastern soft hardwoods	188	205	189	185	147	119	102	73	84	56	22	32	--	1,404
Other eastern hard hardwoods	56	59	63	57	52	30	39	27	11	12	11	--	--	416
Eastern noncommercial hardwoods	32	25	22	16	15	9	3	1	7	3	--	--	--	133
All hardwoods	1,337	1,888	2,273	2,482	2,301	1,969	1,458	1,065	998	475	191	160	77	16,673
All species groups	1,544	2,140	2,541	2,727	2,485	2,064	1,511	1,100	1,011	476	191	160	77	18,026

All table cells without observations in the inventory sample are indicated by --. Table value of 0 indicates the volume rounds to less than 1 million cubic feet. Columns and rows may not add to their totals due to rounding.

Table 16. -- Net volume, in million cubic feet, of all live trees on forest land by forest-type group and stand origin, Missouri, 1999-2003

Forest type group	Stand origin		All forest land
	Natural stands	Artificial regeneration	
White / red / jack pine group	- -	4.8	4.8
Loblolly / shortleaf pine group	245.8	60.5	306.3
Other eastern softwoods group	179.3	0.2	179.5
Exotic softwoods group	- -	0.3	0.3
Oak / pine group	1,017.4	18.7	1,036.0
Oak / hickory group	14,785.7	0.3	14,786.0
Oak / gum / cypress group	96.7	- -	96.7
Elm / ash / cottonwood group	1,512.5	0.3	1,512.7
Maple / beech / birch group	93.0	- -	93.0
Other hardwoods group	2.9	- -	2.9
Exotic hardwoods group	4.2	- -	4.2
Nonstocked	3.7	- -	3.7
All forest type groups	17,941.1	85.0	18,026.1

All table cells without observations in the inventory sample are indicated by -- Table value of 0.0 indicates the volume rounds to less than 0.1 million cubic feet. Columns and rows may not add to their totals due to rounding.

55

Table 17. — Net volume, in million cubic feet, of growing-stock trees on timberland by species group and diameter class, Missouri, 1999-2003

Species group	Diameter class (inches)													All classes
	5.0-6.9	7.0-8.9	9.0-10.9	11.0-12.9	13.0-14.9	15.0-16.9	17.0-18.9	19.0-20.9	21.0-24.9	25.0-28.9	29.0-32.9	33.0-36.9	37.0+	
Softwood species groups														
Eastern softwood species groups														
Loblolly and shortleaf pines	53	102	152	169	130	77	43	28	7	--	--	--	--	761
Other yellow pines	0	0	0	--	--	--	--	--	--	--	--	--	--	1
Eastern white and red pines	0	0	1	2	2	--	--	--	--	--	--	--	--	5
Cypress	--	--	--	0	--	--	--	--	--	--	--	--	--	0
Other eastern softwoods	129	118	84	45	34	10	3	2	2	2	--	--	--	428
All softwoods	182	220	237	216	167	87	46	30	8	2	--	--	--	1,195
Hardwood species groups														
Eastern hardwood species groups														
Select white oaks	228	354	472	556	551	474	318	207	202	64	21	26	--	3,472
Select red oaks	39	62	84	96	128	118	111	110	94	43	9	15	5	915
Other white oaks	149	252	270	240	201	153	79	51	27	6	12	9	--	1,450
Other red oaks	205	331	484	569	552	459	337	229	193	75	22	4	5	3,464
Hickory	186	247	254	258	174	137	75	37	37	13	--	--	--	1,418
Hard maple	33	33	38	28	19	18	13	15	5	--	--	--	--	202
Soft maple	13	17	19	18	20	36	13	23	24	26	--	21	--	229
Beech	--	0	0	--	0	--	--	3	--	--	--	--	--	1
Sweetgum	1	3	3	2	3	3	5	3	--	--	--	--	--	24
Tupelo and blackgum	13	12	11	9	11	7	5	5	6	--	--	--	--	79
Ash	29	39	47	43	40	48	23	19	10	4	--	--	--	301
Cottonwood and aspen	2	2	1	5	1	12	16	22	14	6	12	20	33	145
Basswood	1	2	3	4	2	3	2	5	9	--	--	--	--	32
Yellow-poplar	0	0	1	2	4	3	1	3	--	--	--	--	--	14
Black walnut	20	38	52	72	59	43	49	29	14	16	--	--	--	392
Other eastern soft hardwoods	134	144	138	139	109	94	86	63	62	48	19	20	--	1,056
Other eastern hard hardwoods	30	35	40	29	32	8	17	17	2	4	6	--	--	219
All hardwoods	1,083	1,571	1,917	2,069	1,908	1,618	1,152	835	698	304	100	115	43	13,412
All species groups	1,265	1,791	2,154	2,285	2,074	1,705	1,198	865	706	306	100	115	43	14,607

All table cells without observations in he inventory sample are indicated by --. Table value of 0 indicates the volume rounds to less than 1 million cubic feet. Columns and rows may not add to their totals due to rounding.

56

Table 18. -- Net volume, in million cubic feet, of growing-stock trees on timberland by species group and ownership group, Missouri, 1999-2003

Species group	Ownership group				All owners
	Forest Service	Other Federal	State and local government	Undifferentiated private	
Softwood species groups					
Eastern softwood species groups					
Loblolly and shortleaf pines	376.3	3.3	57.4	324.4	761.3
Other yellow pines	--	--	0.5	0.1	0.6
Eastern white and red pines	--	--	3.1	2.3	5.4
Cypress	--	--	--	0.3	0.3
Other eastern softwoods	27.9	5.1	4.7	389.8	427.5
All softwoods	404.2	8.3	65.7	716.9	1,195.1
Hardwood species groups					
Eastern hardwood species groups					
Select white oaks	445.0	54.9	202.0	2,770.2	3,472.1
Select red oaks	89.1	22.5	57.1	746.6	915.3
Other white oaks	114.5	25.5	41.6	1,268.2	1,449.8
Other red oaks	506.7	35.6	196.6	2,724.9	3,463.8
Hickory	103.8	17.3	69.3	1,227.6	1,418.1
Hard maple	14.8	3.5	6.5	177.3	202.2
Soft maple	2.5	2.4	46.9	176.9	228.7
Beech	--	--	0.2	0.4	0.6
Sweetgum	0.3	3.4	0.4	19.7	23.8
Tupelo and blackgum	16.4	0.3	5.4	57.1	79.2
Ash	7.6	1.8	10.4	281.2	301.0
Cottonwood and aspen	--	3.8	25.8	115.1	144.6
Basswood	1.1	0.2	0.1	30.3	31.8
Yellow-poplar	--	--	3.2	10.6	13.9
Black walnut	13.3	4.3	17.6	356.8	392.1
Other eastern soft hardwoods	31.9	32.2	52.0	939.7	1,055.8
Other eastern hard hardwoods	2.9	2.2	7.9	206.2	219.3
All hardwoods	1,349.9	209.9	743.1	11,109.2	13,412.1
All species groups	1,754.1	218.2	808.8	11,826.1	14,607.3

All table cells without observations in the inventory sample are indicated by --. Table value of 0.0 indicates the volume rounds to less than 0.1 million cubic feet. Columns and rows may not add to their totals due to rounding.

Table 19. – Net volume, in million board feet¹ of sawtimber trees (International 1/4-inch rule) on timberland by species group and diameter class, Missouri, 1999-2003

Species group	Diameter class (inches)											All classes
	9.0-10.9	11.0-12.9	13.0-14.9	15.0-16.9	17.0-18.9	19.0-20.9	21.0-24.9	25.0-28.9	29.0-32.9	33.0-36.9	37.0+	
Softwood species groups												
Eastern softwood species groups												
Loblolly and shortleaf pines	759	868	682	409	231	152	37	--	--	--	--	3,139
Other yellow pines	2	--	--	--	--	--	--	--	--	--	--	2
Eastern white and red pines	3	9	11	--	--	--	--	--	--	--	--	23
Cypress	--	1	--	--	--	--	--	--	--	--	--	1
Other eastern softwoods	464	231	165	48	13	8	7	7	--	--	--	944
All softwoods	1,227	1,110	858	457	245	160	43	7	--	--	--	4,109
Hardwood species groups												
Eastern hardwood species groups												
Select white oaks	--	2,715	2,649	2,238	1,472	937	888	270	83	95	--	11,347
Select red oaks	--	476	639	593	555	546	458	202	39	62	20	3,592
Other white oaks	--	1,170	974	743	377	242	126	27	51	38	--	3,749
Other red oaks	--	2,822	2,748	2,282	1,663	1,117	920	341	95	16	18	12,021
Hickory	--	1,261	854	675	369	182	179	65	--	--	--	3,583
Hard maple	--	133	90	85	63	69	22	--	--	--	--	462
Soft maple	--	79	88	160	56	99	104	108	--	81	--	774
Beech	--	--	2	--	--	--	--	--	--	--	--	2
Sweetgum	--	10	12	16	22	14	--	--	--	--	--	75
Tupelo and blackgum	--	41	51	32	22	21	26	--	--	--	--	193
Ash	--	196	184	226	110	89	46	16	--	--	--	868
Cottonwood and aspen	--	25	6	57	83	109	71	30	56	90	137	665
Basswood	--	20	10	16	10	23	45	--	--	--	--	124
Yellow-poplar	--	8	22	14	4	15	--	--	--	--	--	62
Black walnut	--	342	281	205	232	133	64	65	--	--	--	1,322
Other eastern soft hardwoods	--	635	498	425	385	281	275	211	84	88	--	2,882
Other eastern hard hardwoods	--	135	148	37	79	78	7	15	23	--	--	523
All hardwoods	--	10,069	9,257	7,802	5,503	3,955	3,233	1,351	431	469	175	42,246
All species groups	1,227	11,179	10,115	8,260	5,748	4,115	3,276	1,359	431	469	175	46,355

All table cells without observations in the inventory sample are indicated by --. Table value of 0 indicates the volume rounds to less than 1 million board feet. Columns and rows may not add to their totals due to rounding.
¹ International 1/4-inch rule.

58

Table 19a. -- Net volume, in million board feet[1] of sawtimber trees (Doyle rule) on timberland by species group and diameter class, Missouri, 1999-2003

Species group	Diameter class (inches)											All classes
	9.0-10.9	11.0-12.9	13.0-14.9	15.0-16.9	17.0-18.9	19.0-20.9	21.0-24.9	25.0-28.9	29.0-32.9	33.0-36.9	37.0+	
Softwood species groups												
Eastern softwood species groups												
Loblolly and shortleaf pines	262	415	409	283	178	130	33	--	--	--	--	1,710
Other yellow pines	1	--	--	--	--	--	--	--	--	--	--	1
Eastern white and red pines	1	4	7	--	--	--	--	--	--	--	--	12
Cypress	--	1	--	--	--	--	--	--	--	--	--	1
Other eastern softwoods	160	110	99	33	10	7	6	7	--	--	--	433
All softwoods	424	531	514	316	188	137	39	7	--	--	--	2,156
Hardwood species groups												
Eastern hardwood species groups												
Select white oaks	--	1,133	1,356	1,316	967	673	713	245	95	108	--	6,605
Select red oaks	--	199	327	349	365	392	370	183	45	70	23	2,323
Other white oaks	--	488	499	437	248	173	101	25	58	43	--	2,071
Other red oaks	--	1,177	1,406	1,342	1,092	802	736	303	107	18	20	7,004
Hickory	--	526	437	397	242	131	141	58	--	--	--	1,932
Hard maple	--	55	46	50	41	50	18	--	--	--	--	260
Soft maple	--	33	45	94	37	71	82	100	--	91	--	553
Beech	--	--	1	--	--	--	--	--	--	--	--	1
Sweetgum	--	4	6	9	15	10	--	--	--	--	--	45
Tupelo and blackgum	--	17	26	19	14	15	21	--	--	--	--	113
Ash	--	82	94	133	72	64	37	16	--	--	--	498
Cottonwood and aspen	--	11	3	33	54	78	57	26	64	102	156	585
Basswood	--	8	5	10	7	17	35	--	--	--	--	81
Yellow-poplar	--	3	11	8	3	11	--	--	--	--	--	36
Black walnut	--	143	144	121	152	95	51	60	--	--	--	766
Other eastern soft hardwoods	--	265	255	250	253	202	223	192	95	100	--	1,835
Other eastern hard hardwoods	--	56	76	22	52	56	6	13	26	--	--	307
All hardwoods	--	4,201	4,738	4,589	3,615	2,839	2,590	1,221	490	533	199	25,015
All species groups	424	4,732	5,252	4,905	3,803	2,977	2,629	1,228	490	533	199	27,171

All table cells without observations in the inventory sample are indicated by --. Table value of 0 indicates he volume rounds to less than 1 million board feet. Columns and rows may not add to their totals due to rounding.

[1] Doyle rule.

59

Table 20. – Net volume, in million cubic feet, of sawtimber trees on timberland by species group and ownership group. Missouri, 1999-2003

	Ownership group				
Species group	Forest Service	Other Federal	State and local government	Undifferentiated private	All owners
Softwood species groups					
Eastern softwood species groups					
Loblolly and shortleaf pines	272.0	2.5	38.0	229.4	541.8
Other yellow pines	- -	- -	0.3	- -	0.3
Eastern white and red pines	- -	- -	2.5	1.8	4.4
Cypress	- -	- -	- -	0.3	0.3
Other eastern softwoods	8.9	1.9	1.7	143.4	155.9
All softwoods	280.9	4.4	42.5	374.9	702.7
Hardwood species groups					
Eastern hardwood species groups					
Select white oaks	236.0	42.4	113.2	1,645.2	2,036.8
Select red oaks	59.1	16.1	41.3	528.3	644.8
Other white oaks	52.2	13.5	19.5	539.5	624.8
Other red oaks	331.8	24.4	120.3	1,591.7	2,068.2
Hickory	38.0	4.9	35.5	513.7	592.1
Hard maple	6.3	2.0	2.0	71.9	82.2
Soft maple	0.2	0.2	37.0	124.8	162.3
Beech	- -	- -	- -	0.3	0.3
Sweetgum	- -	1.2	- -	12.8	14.1
Tupelo and blackgum	6.7	- -	2.9	25.3	35.0
Ash	1.9	0.7	5.9	147.3	155.7
Cottonwood and aspen	- -	1.2	25.3	107.0	133.5
Basswood	0.5	- -	- -	22.2	22.7
Yellow-poplar	- -	- -	2.6	8.1	10.7
Black walnut	7.4	1.1	12.9	210.8	232.2
Other eastern soft hardwoods	14.6	23.9	32.3	477.1	547.8
Other eastern hard hardwoods	0.3	- -	4.2	88.6	93.2
All hardwoods	755.1	131.6	455.0	6,114.6	7,456.3
All species groups	1,036.0	136.0	497.4	6,489.5	8,158.9

All table cells without observations in the inventory sample are indicated by --. Table value of 0.0 indicates the volume rounds to less than 0.1 million cubic feet. Columns and rows may not add to their totals due to rounding.

Table 31. -- Live-tree aboveground dry weight (CRM), in thousand dry tons, by owner class and forest land status, Missouri, 1999-2003

Owner class	Unreserved forests			Reserved forests			All forest land
	Timberland	Unproductive	Total	Productive	Unproductive	Total	
Forest Service							
National forest	59,105	269	59,375	3,367	- -	3,367	62,742
Other Federal							
National Park Service	- -	- -	- -	2,991	- -	2,991	2,991
Fish and Wildlife Service	834	- -	834	- -	- -	- -	834
Department of Defense or Energy	1,718	48	1,765	- -	- -	- -	1,765
Other Federal	6,088	89	6,177	1,081	- -	1,081	7,258
State and local government							
State	25,966	160	26,126	4,164	- -	4,164	30,290
Local (county, municipal, etc.)	2,193	- -	2,193	205	- -	205	2,399
Other non-Federal lands	48	- -	48	- -	- -	- -	48
Private							
Undifferentiated private	447,273	7,006	454,279	165	- -	165	454,444
All owners	543,226	7,571	550,797	11,974	- -	11,974	562,771

All table cells without observations in the inventory sample are indicated by --. Table value of 0 indicates the aboveground tree biomass rounds to less than 1 thousand dry tons. Columns and rows may not add to their totals due to rounding.

61

Table 32. — Live-tree aboveground dry weight (CRM), in thousand dry tons, on forest land by species group and diameter class, Missouri, 1999-2003

Species group	Diameter class (inches)															All classes
	1.0-2.9	3.0-4.9	5.0-6.9	7.0-8.9	9.0-10.9	11.0-12.9	13.0-14.9	15.0-16.9	17.0-18.9	19.0-20.9	21.0-22.9	23.0-24.9	25.0-26.9	27.0-28.9	29.0+	
Softwood species groups																
Eastern softwood species groups																
Loblolly and shortleaf pines	69	422	1,165	2,180	3,285	3,613	2,750	1,594	920	627	157	64	--	--	--	16,847
Other yellow pines	--	--	3	5	12	--	--	--	--	--	--	--	--	--	--	20
Eastern white and red pines	--	--	1	8	13	36	42	--	--	--	--	--	--	--	--	100
Cypress	--	--	--	--	--	7	--	--	--	--	--	--	--	--	--	7
Other eastern softwoods	1,053	2,509	3,009	2,850	2,062	1,245	840	310	120	50	--	30	33	--	--	14,112
All softwoods	1,122	2,931	4,178	5,043	5,371	4,901	3,632	1,905	1,041	677	157	94	33	--	--	31,085
Hardwood species groups																
Eastern hardwood species groups																
Select white oaks	1,755	5,666	8,789	12,371	15,914	18,328	18,323	15,578	11,224	7,469	4,673	3,113	1,670	1,472	2,369	128,714
Select red oaks	250	937	1,505	2,251	2,870	3,362	4,149	4,044	3,459	3,595	1,681	1,444	824	484	1,431	32,285
Other white oaks	927	3,101	6,048	9,402	9,997	9,261	7,894	6,424	4,170	2,427	1,212	916	269	333	727	63,109
Other red oaks	2,008	5,052	8,007	11,834	16,317	18,741	17,839	14,958	11,197	7,644	4,579	2,826	2,181	923	1,733	125,837
Hickory	2,952	5,809	7,481	9,337	9,128	8,953	6,327	4,652	2,561	1,415	1,213	312	345	258	153	60,896
Hard maple	739	1,443	1,242	1,140	1,262	1,047	571	690	593	612	115	118	134	--	--	9,707
Soft maple	413	435	442	584	632	725	697	938	440	782	557	289	496	560	1,030	9,020
Beech	0	--	--	2	3	--	21	16	21	--	19	--	--	--	78	161
Sweetgum	16	25	38	76	73	49	71	107	123	90	--	--	--	--	--	669
Tupelo and blackgum	450	630	395	319	282	249	295	166	159	151	84	67	--	--	--	3,246
Ash	608	1,023	1,219	1,587	1,761	1,601	1,416	1,518	704	535	235	38	148	86	--	12,476
Cottonwood and aspen	22	18	35	51	21	112	40	212	333	384	164	82	104	64	1,165	2,806
Basswood	5	14	28	49	68	82	61	49	67	70	149	--	--	--	--	642
Yellow-poplar	4	9	8	12	19	36	82	48	16	77	61	37	--	--	--	410
Black walnut	130	499	771	1,315	1,696	2,211	1,761	1,338	1,329	913	354	99	207	213	330	13,166
Other eastern soft hardwoods	3,042	5,584	5,072	5,168	4,515	4,271	3,337	2,612	2,177	1,549	764	1,061	709	479	1,174	41,512
Other eastern hard hardwoods	2,467	3,268	1,937	1,879	1,942	1,747	1,557	975	1,200	797	197	179	304	120	344	18,912
Eastern noncommercial hardwoods	1,163	1,332	1,310	1,050	922	660	611	414	129	62	138	182	146	--	--	8,119
All hardwoods	16,951	34,845	44,326	58,429	67,419	71,435	65,051	54,737	39,902	28,572	16,195	10,761	7,537	4,992	10,533	531,686
All species groups	18,073	37,776	48,504	63,472	72,791	76,335	68,683	56,641	40,942	29,249	16,353	10,855	7,571	4,992	10,533	562,771

All table cells without observations in the inventory sample are indicated by -- . Table value of 0 indicates the aboveground tree biomass rounds to less than 1 thousand dry tons. Columns and rows may not add to their totals due to rounding.

Table 54. -- Area, in thousand acres, of accessible forest land by Forest Survey Unit, county, and forest land status, Missouri, 1999-2003

Forest Survey Unit and county	Unreserved forests			Reserved forests			All forest land
	Timberland	Unproductive	Total	Productive	Unproductive	Total	
Eastern Ozarks							
Butler	138.4	--	138.4	--	--	--	138.4
Carter	263.0	--	263.0	20.5	--	20.5	283.5
Crawford	299.4	8.2	307.6	--	--	--	307.6
Dent	294.9	4.4	299.4	3.2	--	3.2	302.6
Iron	264.8	13.8	278.6	7.1	--	7.1	285.7
Madison	222.1	--	222.1	--	--	--	222.1
Oregon	271.2	1.0	272.2	35.3	--	35.3	307.5
Reynolds	430.8	--	430.8	3.9	--	3.9	434.7
Ripley	249.0	--	249.0	--	--	--	249.0
St. Francois	150.8	11.5	162.3	9.6	--	9.6	171.9
Shannon	467.5	1.4	468.9	39.1	--	39.1	508.0
Washington	364.8	1.0	365.8	3.2	--	3.2	369.0
Wayne	377.1	2.9	380.1	5.1	--	5.1	385.2
Total	3,793.8	44.3	3,838.1	126.9	--	126.9	3,965.0
Southwestern Ozarks							
Barry	171.3	6.7	178.0	17.1	--	17.1	195.2
Christian	152.8	5.9	158.7	--	--	--	158.7
Douglas	302.2	--	302.2	--	--	--	302.2
Howell	275.9	--	275.9	3.5	--	3.5	279.5
McDonald	166.3	--	166.3	--	--	--	166.3
Newton	120.2	--	120.2	--	--	--	120.2
Ozark	291.1	0.9	292.0	7.1	--	7.1	299.0
Stone	156.9	--	156.9	--	--	--	156.9
Taney	267.0	12.7	279.7	20.3	--	20.3	300.0
Texas	402.4	9.8	412.2	3.5	--	3.5	415.7
Webster	148.8	--	148.8	--	--	--	148.8
Wright	198.3	8.7	207.0	--	--	--	207.0
Total	2,653.3	44.7	2,698.0	51.6	--	51.6	2,749.5

(Table 54 continued on next page)

63

(Table 54 continued)

Forest Survey Unit and county	Unreserved forests			Reserved forests			All forest land
	Timberland	Unproductive	Total	Productive	Unproductive	Total	
Northwestern Ozarks							
Benton	227.9	4.2	232.1	--	--	--	232.1
Camden	250.4	8.4	258.8	6.0	--	6.0	264.8
Cedar	99.5	--	99.5	6.0	--	6.0	105.5
Dallas	169.7	--	169.7	--	--	--	169.7
Hickory	125.9	17.4	143.3	--	--	--	143.3
Laclede	236.4	4.1	240.5	--	--	--	240.5
Maries	142.2	6.6	148.8	--	--	--	148.8
Miller	183.3	11.1	194.4	17.5	--	17.5	211.9
Morgan	183.2	6.8	190.0	--	--	--	190.0
Phelps	218.9	11.8	230.7	--	--	--	230.7
Po k	105.0	--	105.0	--	--	--	105.0
Pulaski	189.8	13.3	203.2	19.3	--	19.3	222.5
St. Clair	160.7	18.7	179.4	--	--	--	179.4
Total	2,293.0	102.4	2,395.4	48.9	--	48.9	2,444.2

(Table 54 continued on next page)

(Table 54 continued)

| | Unreserved forests | | | Reserved forests | | | All |
Forest Survey Unit and county	Timberland	Unproductive	Total	Productive	Unproductive	Total	forest land
Prairie							
Adair	84.7	--	84.7	--	--	--	84.7
Andrew	10.4	--	10.4	--	--	--	10.4
Atchison	20.9	--	20.9	--	--	--	20.9
Audrain	54.2	--	54.2	--	--	--	54.2
Barton	48.9	--	48.9	5.4	--	5.4	54.3
Bates	94.2	--	94.2	--	--	--	94.2
Buchanan	58.0	--	58.0	--	--	--	58.0
Caldwell	20.7	--	20.7	--	--	--	20.7
Carroll	23.3	--	23.3	--	--	--	23.3
Cass	97.1	--	97.1	--	--	--	97.1
Chariton	68.2	--	68.2	--	--	--	68.2
Clark	47.7	5.7	53.5	--	--	--	53.5
Clay	27.9	--	27.9	--	--	--	27.9
Clinton	1.6	--	1.6	--	--	--	1.6
Cooper	68.0	3.2	71.2	--	--	--	71.2
Dade	51.2	--	51.2	--	--	--	51.2
Daviess	54.8	--	54.8	--	--	--	54.8
DeKalb	23.3	--	23.3	--	--	--	23.3
Gentry	58.5	--	58.5	--	--	--	58.5
Greene	80.9	--	80.9	--	--	--	80.9
Grundy	36.7	--	36.7	--	--	--	36.7
Harrison	78.6	--	78.6	--	--	--	78.6
Henry	96.1	--	96.1	--	--	--	96.1
Holt	29.2	--	29.2	--	--	--	29.2
Jackson	75.3	--	75.3	--	--	--	75.3
Jasper	41.9	--	41.9	--	--	--	41.9
Johnson	78.7	--	78.7	6.6	--	6.6	85.3
Knox	43.8	--	43.8	--	--	--	43.8
Lafayette	27.1	--	27.1	--	--	--	27.1
Lawrence	71.7	--	71.7	--	--	--	71.7
Lewis	61.3	--	61.3	--	--	--	61.3
Lincoln	110.5	--	110.5	--	--	--	110.5
Linn	32.5	--	32.5	--	--	--	32.5

(Table 54 continued on next page)

(Table 54 continued)

Forest Survey Unit and county	Unreserved forests			Reserved forests			All forest land
	Timberland	Unproductive	Total	Productive	Unproductive	Total	
Prairie							
Livingston	42.0	--	42.0	--	--	--	42.0
Macon	85.2	3.2	88.4	--	--	--	88.4
Marion	46.2	--	46.2	--	--	--	46.2
Mercer	40.5	--	40.5	--	--	--	40.5
Monroe	106.0	--	106.0	--	--	--	106.0
Nodaway	21.0	--	21.0	--	--	--	21.0
Pettis	50.8	--	50.8	--	--	--	50.8
Pike	126.6	--	126.6	--	--	--	126.6
Platte	45.8	--	45.8	--	--	--	45.8
Putnam	52.4	3.2	55.6	--	--	--	55.6
Ralls	48.6	--	48.6	--	--	--	48.6
Randolph	62.0	--	62.0	--	--	--	62.0
Ray	51.7	--	51.7	--	--	--	51.7
Saline	71.4	--	71.4	6.6	--	6.6	77.9
Schuyler	38.8	--	38.8	--	--	--	38.8
Scotland	53.5	1.2	54.7	--	--	--	54.7
She by	55.1	--	55.1	--	--	--	55.1
Sullivan	78.0	--	78.0	--	--	--	78.0
Vernon	83.0	--	83.0	--	--	--	83.0
Worth	8.2	--	8.2	--	--	--	8.2
Total	2,944.7	16.5	2,961.2	18.5	--	18.5	2,979.7

(Table 54 continued on next page)

(Table 54 continued)

Forest Survey Unit and county	Unreserved forests			Reserved forests			All forest land
	Timberland	Unproductive	Total	Productive	Unproductive	Total	
Riverborder							
Boone	142.1	0.8	142.9	2.2	--	2.2	145.1
Callaway	184.9	4.2	189.1	--	--	--	189.1
Cape Girardeau	85.6	--	85.6	3.1	--	3.1	88.7
Cole	79.9	3.6	83.5	--	--	--	83.5
Dunklin	6.2	--	6.2	--	--	--	6.2
Franklin	245.7	3.9	249.6	8.5	--	8.5	258.1
Gasconade	165.7	6.4	172.1	--	--	--	172.1
Howard	78.2	--	78.2	--	--	--	78.2
Jefferson	217.3	--	217.3	--	--	--	217.3
Mississippi	16.5	--	16.5	--	--	--	16.5
Moniteau	44.1	--	44.1	--	--	--	44.1
Montgomery	92.2	--	92.2	--	--	--	92.2
New Madrid	16.2	--	16.2	--	--	--	16.2
Osage	173.6	0.9	174.5	--	--	--	174.5
Pemiscot	0.8	--	0.8	0.6	--	0.6	1.4
Perry	98.2	2.3	100.5	--	--	--	100.5
St. Charles	79.1	--	79.1	0.7	--	0.7	79.8
Ste. Genevieve	178.8	10.5	189.3	3.1	--	3.1	192.4
St. Louis	53.8	--	53.8	2.2	--	2.2	56.0
Scott	17.1	--	17.1	--	--	--	17.1
Stoddard	40.7	--	40.7	3.1	--	3.1	43.8
Warren	136.8	1.7	138.5	--	--	--	138.5
Total	2,153.5	34.4	2,187.8	23.5	--	23.5	2,211.3
All counties	13,838.2	242.3	14,080.5	269.3	--	269.3	14,349.8

All table cells without observations in the inventory sample are indicated by --. Table value of 0.0 indicates the acres round to less than 0.1 thousand acres. Columns and rows may not add to their totals due to rounding.

67

Table 55. — Area, in thousand acres, of accessible forest land by Forest Survey Unit, county, ownership group, and forest land status, Missouri, 1999-2003

Forest Survey Unit and county	Forest Service		Other Federal		State and local government		Undifferentiated private		All forest land
	Timber-land	Other forest land	Timber-land	Other forest land	Timber-land	Other forest land	Timber-land	Other forest land	
Eastern Ozarks									
Butler	46.1	--	--	--	12.8	--	79.4	--	138.4
Carter	88.0	--	--	16.7	28.7	--	146.2	3.9	283.5
Crawford	36.2	--	--	--	13.5	--	249.7	8.2	307.6
Dent	82.8	2.4	--	--	32.2	4.3	179.9	0.9	302.6
Iron	66.5	14.1	--	--	7.2	2.4	191.1	4.4	285.7
Madison	53.1	--	--	--	--	--	169.0	--	222.1
Oregon	79.8	24.7	--	10.6	--	--	191.4	1.0	307.5
Reynolds	86.0	--	14.7	--	56.4	3.9	273.7	--	434.7
Ripley	88.0	--	--	--	9.6	--	151.4	--	249.0
St. Francois	5.7	--	--	--	6.4	12.8	138.7	8.3	171.9
Shannon	64.2	--	--	38.3	128.3	0.8	275.1	1.4	508.0
Washington	93.8	--	--	--	15.1	3.2	255.9	1.0	369.0
Wayne	93.3	--	30.2	--	16.5	1.7	237.2	6.3	385.2
Total	883.6	41.3	45.0	65.5	326.7	29.1	2,538.5	35.3	3,965.0
Southwestern Ozarks									
Barry	39.3	12.4	--	--	6.6	6.6	125.5	5.0	195.2
Christian	56.2	--	--	--	--	--	96.5	5.9	158.7
Douglas	34.3	--	--	--	6.6	--	261.3	--	302.2
Howell	52.3	3.5	--	--	13.1	--	210.6	--	279.5
McDonald	--	--	--	--	3.3	--	163.0	--	166.3
Newton	--	--	4.0	--	--	--	116.2	--	120.2
Ozark	34.9	7.9	18.9	--	6.6	--	230.7	--	299.0
Stone	14.1	--	3.5	--	6.6	--	132.6	--	156.9
Taney	54.3	20.3	1.3	--	12.9	--	198.4	12.7	300.0
Texas	45.0	3.5	--	--	13.0	--	344.4	9.8	415.7
Webster	--	--	--	--	5.0	--	143.8	--	148.8
Wright	7.1	--	--	--	1.4	--	189.9	8.7	207.0
Total	337.5	47.7	27.8	--	74.9	6.6	2,213.1	42.0	2,749.5

(Table 55 continued on next page)

(Table 55 continued)

Forest Survey Unit and county	Forest Service		Other Federal		State and local government		Undifferentiated private		All forest land
	Timber-land	Other forest land	Timber-land	Other forest land	Timber-land	Other forest land	Timber-land	Other forest land	
Northwestern Ozarks									
Benton	--	--	22.9	--	--	--	205.0	4.2	232.1
Camden	--	--	--	--	--	6.0	250.4	8.4	264.8
Cedar	--	--	--	6.0	--	--	99.5	--	105.5
Dallas	--	--	--	--	6.0	--	163.7	--	169.7
Hickory	--	--	8.3	5.1	14.2	--	103.4	12.3	143.3
Laclede	36.2	--	--	--	6.0	--	194.2	4.1	240.5
Maries	--	--	--	--	--	--	142.2	6.6	148.8
Miller	--	--	--	--	3.2	17.5	180.1	11.1	211.9
Morgan	--	--	--	--	--	--	183.2	6.8	190.0
Phelps	38.8	--	--	--	5.9	--	174.2	11.8	230.7
Polk	--	--	4.8	--	--	--	100.2	--	105.0
Pulaski	53.0	--	25.8	19.3	--	--	111.0	13.3	222.5
St. Clair	--	--	6.2	6.2	--	--	154.5	12.4	179.4
Total	128.1	--	68.0	36.6	35.2	23.5	2,061.7	91.1	2,444.2

(Table 55 continued on next page)

(Table 55 continued)

Prairie

Forest Survey Unit and county	Forest Service		Other Federal		State and local government		Undifferentiated private		All forest land
	Timber-land	Other forest land	Timber-land	Other forest land	Timber-land	Other forest land	Timber-land	Other forest land	
Adair	--	--	--	--	--	--	84.7	--	84.7
Andrew	--	--	--	--	--	--	10.4	--	10.4
Atchison	--	--	7.8	--	7.1	--	6.0	--	20.9
Audrain	--	--	--	--	--	--	54.2	--	54.2
Barton	--	--	--	--	--	5.4	48.9	--	54.3
Bates	--	--	--	--	--	--	94.2	--	94.2
Buchanan	--	--	--	--	--	--	58.0	--	58.0
Caldwell	--	--	--	--	--	--	20.7	--	20.7
Carroll	--	--	--	--	6.1	--	17.2	--	23.3
Cass	--	--	--	--	5.8	--	91.2	--	97.1
Chariton	--	--	--	--	--	--	68.2	--	68.2
Clark	--	--	--	--	--	--	47.7	5.7	53.5
Clay	--	--	2.0	--	8.0	--	17.9	--	27.9
Clinton	--	--	--	--	--	--	1.6	--	1.6
Cooper	--	--	--	--	--	--	68.0	3.2	71.2
Dade	--	--	20.1	--	--	--	31.1	--	51.2
Daviess	--	--	--	--	6.7	--	48.1	--	54.8
DeKalb	--	--	--	--	2.0	--	21.2	--	23.3
Gentry	--	--	--	--	--	--	58.5	--	58.5
Greene	--	--	--	--	6.6	--	74.4	--	80.9
Grundy	--	--	--	--	6.6	--	30.1	--	36.7
Harrison	--	--	17.3	--	--	--	78.6	--	78.6
Henry	--	--	--	--	5.1	--	73.7	--	96.1
Holt	--	--	--	--	--	--	29.2	--	29.2
Jackson	--	--	4.7	--	18.2	--	52.4	--	75.3
Jasper	--	--	--	--	--	--	41.9	--	41.9
Johnson	--	--	--	--	--	6.6	78.7	--	85.3
Knox	--	--	--	--	--	--	43.8	--	43.8
Lafayette	--	--	--	--	--	--	27.1	--	27.1
Lawrence	--	--	--	--	--	--	71.7	--	71.7
Lewis	--	--	--	--	8.2	--	53.2	--	61.3
Lincoln	--	--	--	--	--	--	110.5	--	110.5
Linn	--	--	--	--	--	--	32.5	--	32.5

(Table 55 continued on next page)

(Table 55 continued)

Forest Survey Unit and county	Forest Service		Other Federal		State and local government		Undifferentiated private		All forest land
	Timber-land	Other forest land	Timber-land	Other forest land	Timber-land	Other forest land	Timber-land	Other forest land	
Prairie									
Livingston	--	--	--	--	--	--	42.0	--	42.0
Macon	--	--	6.6	--	6.6	--	72.0	3.2	88.4
Marion	--	--	--	--	--	--	46.2	--	46.2
Mercer	--	--	--	--	--	--	40.5	--	40.5
Monroe	--	--	23.8	--	--	--	82.2	--	106.0
Nodaway	--	--	--	--	--	--	21.0	--	21.0
Pettis	--	--	--	--	--	--	50.8	--	50.8
Pike	--	--	--	--	7.1	--	119.5	--	126.6
Platte	--	--	--	--	3.3	--	42.5	--	45.8
Putnam	--	--	--	--	6.6	--	45.9	3.2	55.6
Ralls	--	--	--	--	--	--	48.6	--	48.6
Randolph	--	--	--	--	--	--	62.0	--	62.0
Ray	--	--	--	--	4.9	--	46.8	--	51.7
Saline	--	--	--	--	6.6	6.6	64.8	--	77.9
Schuyler	--	--	--	--	--	--	38.8	--	38.8
Scotland	--	--	--	--	7.0	--	46.6	1.2	54.7
Shelby	--	--	--	--	7.4	--	47.7	--	55.1
Sullivan	--	--	--	--	12.9	--	65.1	--	78.0
Vernon	--	--	--	--	--	--	83.0	--	83.0
Worth	--	--	--	--	--	--	8.2	--	8.2
Total	--	--	82.4	--	142.7	18.5	2,719.6	16.5	2,979.7

(Table 55 continued on next page)

71

(Table 55 continued)

Forest Survey Unit and county	Forest Service		Other Federal		State and local government		Undifferentiated private		All forest land
	Timber-land	Other forest land	Timber-land	Other forest land	Timber-land	Other forest land	Timber-land	Other forest land	
Riverborder									
Boone	5.3	--	--	--	12.5	2.2	124.2	0.8	145.1
Callaway	12.1	--	--	--	1.7	--	171.1	4.2	189.1
Cape Girardeau	--	--	--	--	3.1	3.1	82.5	--	88.7
Cole	--	--	--	--	--	--	79.9	3.6	83.5
Dunklin	--	--	--	--	1.6	--	4.6	--	6.2
Franklin	--	--	--	--	15.0	8.5	230.7	3.9	258.1
Gasconade	--	--	--	--	--	--	165.7	6.4	172.1
Howard	--	--	2.2	--	2.3	--	73.7	--	78.2
Jefferson	--	--	--	--	3.9	--	213.5	--	217.3
Mississippi	--	--	--	--	3.3	--	13.2	--	16.5
Moniteau	--	--	--	--	--	--	44.1	--	44.1
Montgomery	--	--	--	--	--	--	92.2	--	92.2
New Madrid	--	--	--	--	9.2	--	7.0	--	16.2
Osage	--	--	--	--	--	--	173.6	0.9	174.5
Pemiscot	--	--	--	--	0.8	0.6	--	--	1.4
Perry	--	--	--	--	--	--	98.2	2.3	100.5
St. Charles	--	--	--	--	11.1	0.7	67.9	--	79.8
Ste. Genevieve	13.2	--	--	--	10.4	3.1	155.2	10.5	192.4
St. Louis	--	--	--	--	12.2	2.2	41.6	--	56.0
Scott	--	--	--	--	2.6	--	14.6	--	17.1
Stoddard	--	--	11.6	3.1	2.4	--	26.6	--	43.8
Warren	--	--	--	--	11.5	--	125.3	1.7	138.5
Total	30.6	88.9	13.9	3.1	103.7	20.4	2,005.2	34.4	2,211.3
All counties	1,379.8	88.9	237.0	105.2	683.2	98.1	11,538.2	219.3	14,349.8

All table cells without observations in the inventory sample are indicated by --. Table value of 0.0 indicates the acres round to less than 0.1 thousand acres. Columns and rows may not add to their totals due to rounding.

72

Table 56. – Area, in thousand acres, of forest land by Forest Survey Unit, county/county group, and forest-type group, Missouri, 1999-2003

Forest Survey Unit and county	White-red-jack pine	Loblolly-shortleaf pine	Pinyon-juniper	Exotic softwoods	Oak-pine	Oak-hickory	Oak-gum-cypress	Elm-ash-cottonwood	Maple-beech-birch	Exotic hardwoods	Non-stocked	All groups
Eastern Ozarks												
Butler	--	--	--	--	19.4	92.8	10.2	16.0	--	--	--	138.4
Carter	--	17.3	--	--	26.6	239.6	--	--	--	--	--	283.5
Crawford	--	0.2	--	--	9.1	285.6	--	11.1	--	--	1.7	307.6
Dent	--	5.9	--	--	35.0	261.7	--	--	--	--	--	302.6
Iron	--	4.3	--	--	10.5	264.4	--	--	4.0	--	0.7	285.7
Madison	--	6.4	--	--	13.3	195.9	--	2.0	2.7	--	--	222.1
Oregon	--	3.5	--	--	34.7	260.0	--	7.0	--	--	2.3	307.5
Reynolds	--	4.7	--	--	43.9	365.8	--	11.6	5.5	--	--	434.7
Ripley	--	6.7	--	--	21.0	205.3	--	10.1	3.4	--	--	249.0
St. Francois	--	5.7	--	--	5.2	138.9	--	6.6	--	--	--	171.9
Shannon	--	16.7	--	--	58.1	426.7	--	5.8	0.8	--	--	508.0
Washington	--	6.1	--	--	38.8	312.2	--	4.2	1.0	--	1.0	369.0
Wayne	--	13.4	--	--	27.4	324.9	3.5	5.8	3.5	--	--	385.2
Total	--	90.9	--	--	342.9	3,373.5	13.7	80.0	20.9	--	5.7	3,965.0
Southwestern Ozarks												
Barry	--	6.5	--	--	28.8	153.3	--	--	--	--	--	195.2
Christian	--	--	--	--	15.5	118.7	--	0.8	--	--	--	158.7
Douglas	--	2.6	--	--	11.8	275.6	--	--	--	--	1.1	302.2
Howell	--	14.9	--	--	14.8	242.9	7.0	--	--	--	--	279.5
McDonald	--	--	--	--	1.7	162.6	--	2.0	--	--	--	166.3
Newton	--	--	--	--	--	118.3	--	--	--	--	2.0	120.2
Ozark	--	--	--	--	53.5	229.0	--	8.3	--	--	2.6	299.0
Stone	--	--	--	--	8.3	128.6	--	--	1.6	--	--	156.9
Taney	--	--	--	--	59.7	190.2	--	1.3	--	--	11.8	300.0
Texas	--	30.1	--	--	38.0	342.8	--	--	--	--	--	415.7
Webster	--	--	--	--	10.5	138.3	--	--	--	--	--	148.8
Wright	--	--	--	--	6.9	176.4	--	11.7	--	2.3	--	207.0
Total	--	54.0	--	--	249.4	2,276.7	7.0	24.0	1.6	2.3	17.5	2,749.5

(Table 56 continued on next page)

(Table 56 continued)

Forest Survey Unit and county	Forest type group											
	White-red-jack pine	Loblolly-shortleaf pine	Pinyon-juniper	Exotic softwoods	Oak-pine	Oak-hickory	Oak-gum-cypress	Elm-ash-cottonwood	Maple-beech-birch	Exotic hardwoods	Non-stocked	All groups
Northwestern Ozarks												
Benton	--	--	--	--	16.5	210.2	--	4.4	--	--	--	232.1
Camden	--	--	--	--	--	245.5	--	1.2	1.3	--	13.0	264.8
Cedar	--	--	--	--	6.2	66.2	--	25.3	--	--	3.2	105.5
Dallas	--	--	--	--	8.4	152.4	--	--	--	--	--	169.7
Hickory	--	--	--	--	14.3	116.6	--	--	--	--	--	143.3
Laclede	--	1.8	--	--	12.5	223.4	--	--	--	--	--	240.5
Maries	--	--	--	--	11.3	122.6	--	9.4	--	--	--	148.8
Miller	--	--	--	--	5.8	185.4	2.9	16.0	--	--	1.7	211.9
Morgan	--	--	--	--	--	176.0	--	6.8	--	--	1.7	190.0
Phelps	--	3.5	--	--	20.3	201.2	1.2	--	2.3	--	--	230.7
Polk	--	--	--	--	--	93.5	--	3.0	--	--	2.8	105.0
Pulaski	--	--	--	--	11.3	187.4	--	13.6	6.1	--	4.1	222.5
St. Clair	--	--	--	--	2.1	168.9	--	1.2	--	--	4.6	179.4
Total	--	5.3	--	--	108.9	2,149.3	4.1	81.0	9.8	--	31.2	2,444.2

(Table 56 continued on next page)

74

(Table 56 continued)

Forest Survey Unit and county	White-red-jack pine	Loblolly-shortleaf pine	Pinyon-juniper	Exotic softwoods	Oak-pine	Oak-hickory	Oak-gum-cypress	Elm-ash-cottonwood	Maple-beech-birch	Exotic hardwoods	Non-stocked	All groups
Prairie												
Adair	--	--	--	--	5.8	77.0	--	0.3	--	--	--	84.7
Andrew	--	--	--	--	--	--	--	9.4	1.1	--	--	10.4
Atchison	--	--	--	--	--	8.6	--	12.3	--	--	--	20.9
Audrain	--	--	--	--	--	32.3	7.6	14.3	--	--	--	54.2
Barton	--	--	--	--	--	34.0	--	20.3	--	--	--	54.3
Bates	--	--	--	--	--	61.0	4.9	28.3	--	--	--	94.2
Buchanan	--	--	--	--	--	35.1	--	22.9	--	--	--	58.0
Caldwell	--	--	--	--	--	20.7	--	--	--	--	--	20.7
Carroll	--	--	--	--	--	23.3	--	--	--	--	--	23.3
Cass	--	--	--	--	--	66.1	--	31.0	--	--	--	97.1
Chariton	--	--	--	--	--	44.8	--	23.3	--	--	--	68.2
Clark	--	--	--	--	--	42.0	--	10.0	--	--	--	53.5
Clay	--	--	--	1.4	--	19.9	--	6.6	--	--	--	27.9
Clinton	--	--	--	--	--	1.6	--	--	--	--	--	1.6
Cooper	--	--	--	--	12.0	44.9	--	12.4	--	--	1.9	71.2
Dade	--	--	--	--	--	45.8	--	2.1	--	--	--	51.2
Daviess	--	--	--	--	1.7	46.8	--	1.6	4.8	--	--	54.8
DeKalb	--	--	--	--	--	8.8	--	8.3	--	--	--	23.3
Gentry	--	--	--	--	--	58.5	--	--	--	--	--	58.5
Greene	--	--	--	--	4.3	62.2	7.1	5.9	--	--	--	80.9
Grundy	--	--	--	--	--	30.2	--	6.5	--	--	--	36.7
Harrison	--	--	--	--	--	56.8	--	21.9	--	--	--	78.6
Henry	--	--	--	--	5.6	66.4	4.2	13.2	--	--	--	96.1
Holt	--	--	--	--	--	15.9	--	11.9	--	--	--	29.2
Jackson	--	--	--	--	--	56.8	--	9.3	--	--	6.8	75.3
Jasper	--	--	--	--	--	31.6	--	9.9	--	--	0.4	41.9
Johnson	--	--	--	--	4.2	66.1	--	14.9	--	--	--	85.3
Knox	--	--	--	--	--	24.9	--	17.5	--	--	1.4	43.8
Lafayette	--	--	--	--	--	18.3	--	8.8	--	--	--	27.1
Lawrence	--	--	--	--	--	64.0	--	6.2	--	--	1.5	71.7
Lewis	--	--	--	--	--	55.7	--	5.6	--	--	--	61.3
Lincoln	--	--	--	--	--	98.5	--	2.0	5.9	--	4.1	110.5
Linn	--	--	--	--	--	31.9	--	0.5	--	--	--	32.5
Livingston	--	--	--	--	5.2	26.3	--	10.5	--	--	--	42.0
Macon	--	--	--	--	--	72.2	--	16.2	--	--	--	88.4
Marion	--	--	--	--	--	41.9	--	4.3	--	--	--	46.2
Mercer	--	--	--	--	--	35.8	--	4.7	--	--	--	40.5
Monroe	--	--	--	--	0.7	80.2	--	25.0	--	--	--	106.0
Nodaway	--	--	--	--	--	18.8	--	0.6	--	--	1.6	21.0

(Table 56 continued on next page)

75

(Table 56 continued)

Forest Survey Unit and county	White-red-jack pine	Loblolly-shortleaf pine	Piñon-juniper	Exotic softwoods	Oak-pine	Oak-hickory	Oak-gum-cypress	Elm-ash-cottonwood	Maple-beech-birch	Exotic hardwoods	Non-stocked	All groups
Prairie												
Pet is	--	--	--	--	--	48.0	--	2.8	--	--	--	50.8
Pike	--	--	--	--	--	106.2	--	20.5	--	--	--	126.6
Platte	--	--	--	--	--	38.0	--	7.8	--	--	--	45.8
Putnam	--	--	--	--	--	50.8	--	4.8	--	--	--	55.6
Ralls	--	--	--	--	5.9	42.7	--	--	--	--	--	48.6
Randolph	--	--	--	--	--	62.0	--	--	--	--	--	62.0
Ray	--	--	--	--	--	42.6	--	7.7	--	--	1.4	51.7
Saline	--	--	--	--	--	60.6	--	17.4	--	--	--	77.9
Schuyler	--	--	--	--	--	38.8	--	--	--	--	--	38.8
Scotland	--	--	--	--	--	36.6	--	18.0	--	--	--	54.7
Shelby	--	--	--	--	--	32.4	--	17.7	--	--	5.1	55.1
Sullivan	--	--	--	--	--	54.9	--	17.3	--	--	--	78.0
Vernon	--	--	--	--	--	35.4	--	47.5	--	--	--	83.0
Worth	--	--	--	--	--	8.2	--	--	--	--	--	8.2
Total	--	--	--	1.4	45.4	2,282.9	23.8	559.6	11.8	--	24.2	2,979.7
Riverborder												
Boone	--	--	--	--	15.6	111.0	--	13.3	--	--	--	145.1
Callaway	--	--	--	--	15.9	150.3	0.9	13.3	--	--	--	189.1
Cape Girardeau	--	--	--	--	2.5	65.5	--	11.9	8.8	--	--	88.7
Cole	--	--	--	--	6.7	64.0	--	1.7	--	--	--	83.5
Dunklin	--	--	--	--	--	3.1	--	3.1	--	--	--	6.2
Franklin	--	--	--	--	33.9	201.2	0.8	6.1	--	--	4.2	258.1
Gasconade	--	--	--	--	12.8	143.9	--	5.1	--	--	3.9	172.1
Howard	--	--	--	--	4.2	59.5	--	14.6	--	--	--	78.2
Jefferson	--	--	--	--	21.9	161.2	--	5.9	1.0	--	0.4	217.3
Mississippi	--	--	--	--	--	--	--	16.5	--	--	--	16.5
Moniteau	--	--	--	--	2.3	37.5	--	1.2	--	--	3.0	44.1
Montgomery	--	--	--	--	4.0	77.7	--	1.0	--	--	--	92.2
New Madrid	--	--	--	--	--	--	2.8	13.1	--	--	3.1	16.2
Osage	--	--	--	--	16.9	150.3	--	5.6	--	--	--	174.5
Pemiscot	--	--	--	--	--	--	--	0.6	--	--	0.8	1.4
Perry	--	--	--	--	4.0	90.5	--	5.2	--	--	--	100.5
St. Charles	--	--	--	--	--	48.8	--	16.0	8.0	--	--	79.8
Ste. Genevieve	--	3.5	--	--	28.9	137.3	--	5.0	3.7	--	1.0	192.4
St. Louis	--	--	--	--	--	47.4	--	5.9	--	--	2.8	56.0
Scott	--	--	--	--	--	11.1	3.4	2.7	--	--	--	17.1
Stoddard	--	3.2	--	--	--	23.3	12.9	4.4	--	--	--	43.8
Warren	1.5	--	--	--	--	123.6	--	4.5	6.6	--	--	138.5
Total	1.5	6.8	--	--	169.6	1,707.5	20.8	156.6	28.1	--	19.1	2,211.3
All counties	1.5	156.9	--	1.4	916.1	11,789.9	69.4	901.2	72.1	2.3	97.8	14,349.8

All table cells without observations in the inventory sample are indicated by --. Table value of 0.0 indicates the acres round to less

(Table 56 continued)

Forest Survey Unit and county	Forest type group										
	White-red-jack pine	Loblolly-shortleaf pine	Pinyon-juniper	Exotic softwoods	Oak-pine	Oak-hickory	Oak-gum-cypress	Elm-ash-cottonwood	Maple-beech-birch	Exotic hardwoods	Non-stocked	All groups

than 0.1 thousand acres. Columns and rows may not add to their totals due to rounding.

Table 57. -- Area, in thousand acres, of timberland by Forest Survey Unit, county, and stand-size class, Missouri, 1999-2003

Forest Survey Unit and county	Large diameter	Medium diameter	Small diameter	Chaparral	Nonstocked	All size classes
Eastern Ozarks						
Butler	83.5	46.7	8.2	--	--	138.4
Carter	130.5	110.8	21.7	--	--	263.0
Crawford	141.0	126.6	30.0	--	1.7	299.4
Dent	149.3	116.5	29.1	--	--	294.9
Iron	125.7	117.7	20.6	--	0.7	264.8
Madison	124.3	82.2	15.6	--	--	222.1
Oregon	143.0	100.2	25.7	--	2.3	271.2
Reynolds	213.3	182.0	35.5	--	--	430.8
Ripley	111.4	116.6	20.9	--	--	249.0
St. Francois	66.7	64.5	19.6	--	--	150.8
Shannon	217.8	184.0	65.8	--	--	467.5
Washington	185.6	129.2	48.9	--	1.0	364.8
Wayne	185.6	159.3	32.3	--	--	377.1
Total	1,877.7	1,536.3	374.1	--	5.7	3,793.8
Southwestern Ozarks						
Barry	102.6	57.6	11.1	--	--	171.3
Christian	57.9	61.9	32.9	--	--	152.8
Douglas	106.3	125.0	69.9	--	1.1	302.2
Howell	109.4	156.4	10.1	--	--	275.9
McDonald	100.9	52.2	13.2	--	--	166.3
Newton	87.3	23.0	7.9	--	2.0	120.2
Ozark	112.8	117.2	58.5	--	2.6	291.1
Stone	37.7	96.1	23.0	--	--	156.9
Taney	115.1	105.2	34.8	--	11.8	267.0
Texas	154.9	194.0	53.5	--	--	402.4
Webster	83.1	45.3	20.4	--	--	148.8
Wright	99.3	69.2	29.8	--	--	198.3
Total	1,167.4	1,103.2	365.2	--	17.5	2,653.3

(Table 57 continued on next page)

(Table 57 continued)

Forest Survey Unit and county	Stand-size class					All size classes
	Large diameter	Medium diameter	Small diameter	Chaparral	Nonstocked	
Northwestern Ozarks						
Benton	127.4	100.5	0.0	--	--	227.9
Camden	138.4	71.5	27.5	--	13.0	250.4
Cedar	48.5	33.3	14.5	--	3.2	99.5
Dallas	91.8	55.8	22.1	--	--	169.7
Hickory	53.0	70.9	2.0	--	--	125.9
Laclede	137.7	90.2	8.4	--	--	236.4
Maries	72.1	68.7	1.4	--	--	142.2
Miller	67.5	91.8	22.3	--	1.7	183.3
Morgan	104.0	66.5	11.0	--	1.7	183.2
Phelps	76.0	124.2	18.8	--	--	218.9
Polk	48.7	38.0	15.5	--	2.8	105.0
Pulaski	71.9	89.9	24.0	--	4.1	189.8
St. Clair	70.6	75.9	9.6	--	4.6	160.7
Total	1,107.5	977.1	177.2	--	31.2	2,293.0

(Table 57 continued on next page)

(Table 57 continued)

Forest Survey Unit and county	Stand-size class					All size classes
	Large diameter	Medium diameter	Small diameter	Chaparral	Nonstocked	
Prairie						
Adair	25.4	31.3	28.0	--	--	84.7
Andrew	8.7	1.8	--	--	--	10.4
Atchison	13.1	5.8	2.0	--	--	20.9
Audrain	42.9	11.4	--	--	--	54.2
Barton	20.5	28.4	--	--	--	48.9
Bates	42.9	27.4	23.9	--	--	94.2
Buchanan	32.9	25.1	--	--	--	58.0
Caldwell	6.7	10.1	3.9	--	--	20.7
Carroll	5.0	8.6	9.7	--	--	23.3
Cass	30.0	54.1	13.0	--	--	97.1
Chariton	34.3	20.5	13.4	--	--	68.2
Clark	29.8	14.7	3.3	--	--	47.7
Clay	16.8	7.8	3.3	--	--	27.9
Clinton	1.6	--	--	--	--	1.6
Cooper	19.9	28.8	17.4	--	1.9	68.0
Dade	35.0	11.5	4.7	--	--	51.2
Daviess	37.2	15.9	1.7	--	--	54.8
DeKalb	3.6	10.4	9.3	--	--	23.3
Gentry	39.1	14.7	4.7	--	--	58.5
Greene	48.3	25.6	7.1	--	--	80.9
Grundy	24.8	11.9	--	--	--	36.7
Harrison	40.9	23.3	14.5	--	--	78.6
Henry	40.0	47.0	9.0	--	--	96.1
Holt	22.0	7.2	--	--	--	29.2
Jackson	45.5	12.0	11.0	--	6.8	75.3
Jasper	8.0	16.4	17.1	--	0.4	41.9
Johnson	39.0	24.6	15.1	--	--	78.7
Knox	27.3	12.1	3.0	--	1.4	43.8
Lafayette	11.6	14.0	1.5	--	--	27.1
Lawrence	31.3	12.3	26.6	--	1.5	71.7
Lewis	37.3	11.2	12.8	--	--	61.3
Lincoln	61.2	33.5	11.6	--	4.1	110.5
Linn	8.3	17.6	6.5	--	--	32.5

(Table 57 continued on next page)

(Table 57 continued)

Forest Survey Unit and county	Stand-size class					All size classes
	Large diameter	Medium diameter	Small diameter	Chaparral	Nonstocked	
Prairie						
Livingston	30.7	11.3	--	--	--	42.0
Macon	35.3	45.6	4.4	--	--	85.2
Marion	40.4	5.7	--	--	--	46.2
Mercer	26.9	1.6	12.0	--	--	40.5
Monroe	40.8	44.7	20.5	--	--	106.0
Nodaway	13.9	5.6	--	--	1.6	21.0
Pettis	20.4	11.7	18.7	--	--	50.8
Pike	77.5	47.7	1.4	--	--	126.6
Platte	19.7	26.1	--	--	--	45.8
Putnam	26.6	24.2	1.6	--	--	52.4
Ralls	21.5	11.6	15.5	--	--	48.6
Randolph	48.9	7.3	5.9	--	--	62.0
Ray	33.3	16.9	--	--	1.4	51.7
Saline	51.4	20.0	--	--	--	71.4
Schuyler	21.2	17.7	--	--	--	38.8
Scotland	23.7	19.7	10.2	--	--	53.5
Shelby	23.3	14.8	12.0	--	5.1	55.1
Sullivan	43.6	14.4	19.9	--	--	78.0
Vernon	56.5	16.2	10.2	--	--	83.0
Worth	6.7	1.5	--	--	--	8.2
Total	1,553.0	961.2	406.3	--	24.2	2,944.7

(Table 57 continued on next page)

81

(Table 57 continued)

Forest Survey Unit and county	Stand-size class					All size classes
	Large diameter	Medium diameter	Small diameter	Chaparral	Nonstocked	
Riverborder						
Boone	82.0	43.0	17.1	--	--	142.1
Callaway	109.4	61.0	14.4	--	--	184.9
Cape Girardeau	75.0	9.7	0.8	--	--	85.6
Cole	42.7	23.3	13.9	--	--	79.9
Dunklin	6.2	--	--	--	--	6.2
Franklin	185.2	42.2	14.0	--	4.2	245.7
Gasconade	90.5	57.8	13.5	--	3.9	165.7
Howard	40.5	29.5	8.3	--	--	78.2
Jefferson	119.6	85.3	12.1	--	0.4	217.3
Mississippi	11.4	5.1	--	--	--	16.5
Moniteau	21.5	9.7	9.9	--	3.0	44.1
Montgomery	60.5	24.3	7.4	--	--	92.2
New Madrid	7.0	6.1	--	--	3.1	16.2
Osage	92.2	69.6	11.7	--	--	173.6
Pemiscot	--	--	--	--	0.8	0.8
Perry	65.2	29.9	3.0	--	--	98.2
St. Charles	51.3	18.3	9.5	--	--	79.1
Ste. Genevieve	106.8	56.4	14.6	--	1.0	178.8
St. Louis	37.7	10.0	3.3	--	2.8	53.8
Scott	14.2	0.1	2.7	--	--	17.1
Stoddard	13.1	15.9	11.8	--	--	40.7
Warren	110.7	23.1	3.0	--	--	136.8
Total	1,342.8	620.5	171.1	--	19.1	2,153.5
All counties	7,048.3	5,198.2	1,493.9	--	97.8	13,838.2

All table cells without observations in the inventory sample are indicated by --. Table value of 0.0 indicates the acres round to less than 0.1 thousand acres. Columns and rows may not add to their totals due to rounding.

Table 58 -- Area, in thousand acres, of timberland by Forest Survey Unit, county, and stocking class, Missouri, 1999-2003

Forest Survey Unit and county	Nonstocked	Poorly stocked	Moderately stocked	Fully stocked	Over-stocked	All classes
Eastern Ozarks						
Butler	0.7	18.0	49.2	69.7	0.7	138.4
Carter	- -	17.3	139.2	102.5	4.1	263.0
Crawford	4.0	27.3	147.5	109.4	11.1	299.4
Dent	0.4	36.2	131.9	117.2	9.2	294.9
Iron	0.7	30.2	121.3	106.0	6.6	264.8
Madison	2.9	22.8	100.6	90.3	5.5	222.1
Oregon	5.6	60.6	118.7	77.7	8.6	271.2
Reynolds	0.8	70.5	220.3	131.6	7.6	430.8
Ripley	1.3	24.8	112.3	99.6	10.9	249.0
St. Francois	0.5	22.3	52.0	72.4	3.6	150.8
Shannon	1.0	47.1	254.5	149.8	15.1	467.5
Washington	1.5	39.0	135.6	168.3	20.5	364.8
Wayne	- -	38.7	190.7	139.0	8.7	377.1
Total	19.5	454.7	1,773.8	1,433.6	112.2	3,793.8
Southwestern Ozarks						
Barry	0.2	31.6	76.6	58.4	4.6	171.3
Christian	14.3	36.7	42.5	57.0	2.2	152.8
Douglas	12.9	59.7	174.2	45.5	9.9	302.2
Howell	7.8	38.5	85.4	142.6	1.7	275.9
McDonald	- -	20.4	69.6	72.3	4.0	166.3
Newton	4.9	11.5	27.8	71.5	4.5	120.2
Ozark	14.7	85.7	91.0	88.4	11.3	291.1
Stone	- -	36.8	58.6	57.7	3.8	156.9
Taney	14.7	58.0	127.5	66.8	- -	267.0
Texas	2.0	47.2	185.7	163.0	4.6	402.4
Webster	0.7	23.1	63.7	61.2	- -	148.8
Wright	2.3	57.3	83.5	55.2	- -	198.3
Total	74.5	506.5	1,086.0	939.5	46.6	2,653.3

(Table 58 continued on next page)

83

(Table 58 continued)

Forest Survey Unit and county	Stocking class of growing-stock trees					All classes
	Nonstocked	Poorly stocked	Moderately stocked	Fully stocked	Over-stocked	
Northwestern Ozarks						
Benton	1.0	48.2	76.4	102.3	--	227.9
Camden	13.0	46.0	126.9	64.4	--	250.4
Cedar	3.2	34.6	43.9	16.7	1.2	99.5
Dallas	--	37.4	88.2	42.9	1.2	169.7
Hickory	--	45.0	66.8	14.1	--	125.9
Laclede	6.5	54.3	102.4	71.3	1.8	236.4
Maries	2.1	28.8	58.4	52.9	--	142.2
Miller	13.7	34.5	71.4	55.1	8.7	183.3
Morgan	4.8	46.5	76.4	54.2	1.3	183.2
Phelps	5.9	43.7	90.6	70.3	8.4	218.9
Polk	8.3	19.3	45.7	18.2	13.5	105.0
Pulaski	5.6	23.1	81.4	75.9	3.9	189.8
St. Clair	13.9	35.3	74.0	36.8	0.8	160.7
Total	78.0	496.8	1,002.5	675.0	40.8	2,293.0

(Table 58 continued on next page)

84

(Table 58 continued)

Forest Survey Unit and county	Stocking class of growing-stock trees					All classes
	Nonstocked	Poorly stocked	Moderately stocked	Fully stocked	Over-stocked	
Prairie						
Adair	0.9	19.0	30.8	33.7	0.2	84.7
Andrew	0.9	0.7	5.6	1.4	1.8	10.4
Atchison	1.5	7.3	2.0	10.1	--	20.9
Audrain	--	9.7	20.7	23.9	--	54.2
Barton	--	22.2	23.9	2.8	--	48.9
Bates	21.4	28.9	23.7	20.2	--	94.2
Buchanan	5.7	27.6	21.2	1.4	2.0	58.0
Caldwell	6.7	5.0	5.0	3.9	--	20.7
Carroll	9.3	13.9	--	--	--	23.3
Cass	15.5	18.5	32.6	30.5	--	97.1
Chariton	8.5	--	35.3	23.4	1.0	68.2
Clark	2.6	20.5	17.4	7.2	--	47.7
Clay	--	3.5	11.1	13.3	--	27.9
Clinton	--	1.6	--	--	--	1.6
Cooper	8.3	14.8	15.9	25.3	3.6	68.0
Dade	0.5	10.8	18.2	19.6	2.1	51.2
Daviess	1.9	13.6	21.0	18.4	--	54.8
DeKalb	--	9.8	3.6	6.7	3.1	23.3
Gentry	--	25.6	20.2	8.0	4.7	58.5
Greene	5.3	12.0	24.5	39.2	--	80.9
Grundy	7.1	11.1	16.9	1.6	--	36.7
Harrison	--	22.8	39.7	16.1	--	78.6
Henry	10.6	47.0	25.7	8.9	3.8	96.1
Holt	--	16.8	5.9	6.6	--	29.2
Jackson	17.5	15.8	30.9	9.3	1.8	75.3
Jasper	0.4	2.3	24.1	15.1	--	41.9
Johnson	2.4	20.5	26.9	28.8	--	78.7
Knox	3.1	12.9	15.7	12.1	--	43.8
Lafayette	--	8.1	17.6	--	1.5	27.1
Lawrence	7.4	5.5	27.5	17.7	13.6	71.7
Lewis	5.9	4.3	31.0	20.1	--	61.3
Lincoln	4.1	12.6	49.0	37.1	7.7	110.5
Linn	0.5	11.3	6.4	7.9	6.4	32.5

(Table 58 continued on next page)

85

(Table 58 continued)

Forest Survey Unit and county	Stocking class of growing-stock trees					
	Nonstocked	Poorly stocked	Moderately stocked	Fully stocked	Over- stocked	All classes
Prairie						
Livingston	5.4	10.3	20.2	6.1	--	42.0
Macon	6.6	21.1	24.6	32.0	1.0	85.2
Marion	--	8.9	25.2	10.6	1.4	46.2
Mercer	7.7	14.9	6.7	11.2	--	40.5
Monroe	--	40.6	36.3	29.1	--	106.0
Nodaway	3.1	12.7	5.2	--	--	21.0
Pettis	0.7	17.0	4.7	28.1	0.4	50.8
Pike	1.6	22.5	80.9	21.7	--	126.6
Platte	1.4	24.4	12.1	7.8	--	45.8
Putnam	4.8	21.8	17.8	6.4	1.6	52.4
Ralls	5.9	--	38.8	3.8	--	48.6
Randolph	0.8	11.0	20.7	29.5	--	62.0
Ray	13.1	3.9	20.8	13.8	--	51.7
Saline	4.3	12.0	30.5	23.5	1.1	71.4
Schuyler	6.4	--	26.0	6.4	--	38.8
Scotland	6.3	18.9	24.4	3.9	--	53.5
She by	9.7	5.7	26.4	13.3	--	55.1
Sullivan	4.4	17.5	27.6	28.5	--	78.0
Vernon	3.5	37.7	20.5	16.7	4.5	83.0
Worth	1.5	1.7	5.0	--	--	8.2
Total	235.5	758.7	1,124.5	762.6	63.4	2,944.7

(Table 58 continued on next page)

86

(Table 58 continued)

Forest Survey Unit and county	Stocking class of growing-stock trees					All classes
	Nonstocked	Poorly stocked	Moderately stocked	Fully stocked	Over-stocked	
Riverborder						
Boone	1.0	26.7	70.6	41.3	2.5	142.1
Callaway	1.4	28.3	89.4	54.5	11.3	184.9
Cape Girardeau	3.3	5.0	39.6	36.9	0.8	85.6
Cole	--	8.0	40.4	28.1	3.4	79.9
Dunklin	--	5.5	--	--	0.7	6.2
Franklin	4.8	38.2	94.2	103.8	4.7	245.7
Gasconade	4.5	17.9	71.6	58.2	13.5	165.7
Howard	0.7	16.4	42.3	11.6	7.2	78.2
Jefferson	3.5	26.7	84.2	102.4	0.5	217.3
Mississippi	0.6	10.9	--	3.3	1.6	16.5
Moniteau	4.3	10.4	14.2	13.7	1.5	44.1
Montgomery	2.2	20.2	41.7	26.4	1.7	92.2
New Madrid	3.1	3.1	7.0	3.1	--	16.2
Osage	3.8	24.0	74.6	70.4	0.9	173.6
Pemiscot	0.8	--	--	--	--	0.8
Perry	--	6.1	52.3	33.4	6.4	98.2
St. Charles	0.6	6.6	29.8	40.5	1.6	79.1
Ste. Genevieve	1.8	33.0	68.7	74.4	0.8	178.8
St. Louis	2.8	6.4	17.5	27.0	--	53.8
Scott	0.3	5.0	5.8	5.9	--	17.1
Stoddard	0.1	5.1	16.4	16.0	3.1	40.7
Warren	1.5	6.5	59.4	65.3	4.1	136.8
Total	41.1	309.9	919.9	816.2	66.3	2,153.5
All counties	448.5	2,526.6	5,906.7	4,627.0	329.3	13,838.2

All table cells without observations in the inventory sample are indicated by --. Table value of 0.0 indicates the acres round to less than 0.1 thousand acres. Columns and rows may not add to their totals due to rounding.

Table 59. -- Net volume of growing-stock and sawtimber (International 1/4-inch rule) on timberland by Forest Survey Unit, county, and major species group, Missouri, 1999-2003

	Growing stock					Sawtimber				
	Major species group					Major species group				
Forest Survey Unit and county	Pine	Other softwoods	Soft hardwoods	Hard hardwoods	All species	Pine	Other softwoods	Soft hardwoods	Hard hardwoods	All species
	In million cubic feet					In million board feet [1]				
Eastern Ozarks										
Butler	19.2	0.3	20.6	135.8	176.0	80.0	1.4	52.2	457.5	591.2
Carter	61.7	1.1	9.5	226.5	298.8	231.8	4.8	19.9	672.6	929.1
Crawford	1.3	5.8	24.7	277.2	309.0	3.3	14.7	76.1	856.9	951.0
Dent	28.9	1.9	4.0	252.2	287.1	124.0	2.4	8.9	707.3	842.6
Iron	19.0	2.8	7.4	253.8	283.0	78.9	6.7	10.3	741.3	837.3
Madison	28.1	4.5	10.6	215.9	259.1	112.7	8.6	21.7	718.1	861.1
Oregon	39.3	0.9	3.8	230.7	274.7	172.2	2.1	6.3	726.0	906.6
Reynolds	70.8	3.0	20.9	362.4	457.1	291.1	7.3	60.2	1,065.7	1,424.2
Ripley	45.2	2.0	21.9	210.5	279.6	214.8	4.5	48.7	592.2	860.3
St. Francois	11.2	8.7	10.0	123.7	153.6	37.1	16.6	26.4	376.3	456.5
Shannon	82.9	4.9	14.7	395.4	497.9	328.7	13.0	37.4	1,198.1	1,577.1
Washington	54.6	7.6	10.5	329.5	402.2	247.0	12.8	21.3	1,011.6	1,292.7
Wayne	66.3	2.0	23.5	355.7	447.5	278.3	4.6	51.8	1,077.8	1,412.5
Total	528.5	45.6	182.1	3,369.3	4,125.5	2,200.0	99.6	441.2	10,201.3	12,942.1
Southwestern Ozarks										
Barry	14.1	13.7	5.9	168.2	201.9	52.2	20.3	11.2	573.1	656.8
Christian	2.7	9.1	7.8	104.4	123.9	12.3	10.4	28.3	305.5	356.5
Douglas	19.6	4.9	7.2	187.9	219.7	91.4	7.3	20.9	534.5	654.1
Howell	37.8	0.3	3.3	262.9	304.2	162.6	- -	8.1	726.1	896.9
McDonald	3.5	3.2	8.2	170.8	185.7	17.9	10.9	6.4	567.0	602.2
Newton	- -	1.3	4.0	178.2	183.6	- -	4.5	- -	704.5	709.0
Ozark	18.8	12.5	15.0	180.8	227.1	88.8	14.6	35.2	549.9	688.5
Stone	- -	22.6	3.5	95.5	121.5	- -	50.5	7.8	239.6	298.0
Taney	5.2	39.3	6.5	153.6	204.6	10.3	77.7	9.3	456.4	553.6
Texas	82.2	3.9	10.7	302.6	399.4	313.3	2.5	6.4	816.7	1,138.9
Webster	- -	1.6	5.1	158.2	164.9	- -	- -	12.2	549.2	561.4
Wright	0.4	5.6	28.9	143.1	178.0	- -	7.5	99.7	450.3	557.5
Total	184.3	118.0	106.1	2,106.3	2,514.6	748.8	206.3	245.4	6,472.7	7,673.3

(Table 59 continued on next page)

88

(Table 59 continued)

Forest Survey Unit and county	Growing stock					Sawtimber					
	Major species group					Major species group					
	Pine	Other softwoods	Soft hardwoods	Hard hardwoods	All species	Pine	Other softwoods	Soft hardwoods	Hard hardwoods	All species
	In million cubic feet					In million board feet [1]					
Northwestern Ozarks										
Benton	- -	10.4	9.3	216.3	236.0	- -	22.9	25.7	639.9	688.5
Camden	- -	2.1	1.9	203.1	207.1	- -	- -	4.0	676.5	680.6
Cedar	- -	3.7	58.6	49.7	111.9	- -	12.0	217.3	141.5	370.8
Dallas	- -	9.0	10.2	130.3	149.5	- -	19.9	26.0	403.3	449.2
Hickory	- -	8.7	2.1	78.3	89.1	- -	11.5	2.7	206.4	220.5
Laclede	7.5	5.6	9.3	201.5	223.9	25.2	11.2	29.0	623.6	689.1
Maries	- -	13.6	4.2	123.8	141.5	- -	22.1	9.7	358.7	390.5
Miller	- -	4.0	8.6	152.3	164.9	- -	7.3	18.4	469.7	495.4
Morgan	- -	1.7	7.2	183.9	192.8	- -	2.0	20.2	574.6	596.8
Phelps	7.2	7.3	3.7	155.7	173.9	31.6	13.6	7.4	378.4	431.0
Polk	- -	4.7	10.1	71.9	86.7	- -	5.7	30.8	201.4	237.9
Pulaski	1.2	4.0	32.3	156.5	194.0	4.6	8.0	112.2	428.1	553.0
St. Clair	- -	2.4	10.8	118.0	131.1	- -	3.9	29.8	339.5	373.2
Total	15.9	77.0	168.3	1,841.3	2,102.5	61.4	140.1	533.4	5,441.5	6,176.4

(Table 59 continued on next page)

89

(Table 59 continued)

Forest Survey Unit and county	Growing stock					Sawtimber				
	Major species group					Major species group				
	Pine	Other softwoods	Soft hardwoods	Hard hardwoods	All species	Pine	Other softwoods	Soft hardwoods	Hard hardwoods	All species
	In million cubic feet					In million board feet[1]				
Prairie										
Adair	--	0.2	4.0	54.6	58.7	--	--	2.2	148.2	150.4
Andrew	--	--	27.5	5.6	33.1	--	--	116.9	21.5	138.3
Atchison	--	--	12.2	15.0	27.1	--	--	39.4	66.7	106.1
Audrain	--	--	23.1	61.0	84.2	--	--	76.8	184.9	261.7
Barton	--	--	11.0	40.7	51.8	--	--	24.0	159.4	183.4
Bates	--	0.1	21.4	36.9	58.4	--	--	67.5	127.9	195.4
Buchanan	--	--	36.4	20.4	56.8	--	--	133.0	67.2	200.1
Caldwell	--	--	4.0	3.9	7.9	--	--	10.4	6.9	17.3
Carroll	--	--	0.5	2.8	3.3	--	--	--	8.4	8.4
Cass	--	0.6	26.6	60.9	88.1	--	1.4	58.6	216.4	276.4
Chariton	--	0.5	12.0	48.9	61.4	--	1.7	27.5	146.6	175.7
Clark	--	1.2	5.5	27.4	34.1	--	2.8	7.5	96.1	106.4
Clay	0.3	--	19.3	18.4	38.0	1.7	--	63.9	68.2	133.7
Clinton	--	--	--	1.1	1.1	--	--	--	5.1	5.1
Cooper	--	3.0	10.1	42.8	55.9	--	2.6	30.9	143.4	176.8
Dade	--	0.1	12.4	45.8	58.3	--	--	35.0	154.7	189.7
Daviess	--	--	9.5	55.3	64.9	--	--	35.0	191.6	226.6
DeKalb	--	--	6.8	7.3	14.2	--	--	18.5	27.3	45.7
Gentry	--	--	9.6	49.9	59.4	--	--	27.8	177.6	205.4
Greene	--	1.9	13.8	85.5	101.2	--	3.0	44.3	318.4	365.7
Grundy	--	--	10.6	14.7	25.3	--	--	42.9	36.1	79.0
Harrison	--	0.1	12.7	51.6	64.4	--	--	31.9	181.2	213.1
Henry	--	4.7	23.4	45.1	73.2	--	12.1	92.3	128.5	232.9
Holt	--	0.0	6.5	16.4	22.9	--	--	18.1	59.1	77.2
Jackson	--	--	51.5	41.1	92.6	--	--	203.1	145.8	349.0
Jasper	--	--	11.1	25.2	36.4	--	--	18.3	89.7	108.0
Johnson	--	0.2	10.9	62.2	73.2	--	--	32.9	189.8	222.8
Knox	--	0.1	8.9	29.1	38.1	--	--	26.2	90.7	116.9
Lafayette	--	--	5.5	14.3	19.8	--	--	9.0	54.1	63.1
Lawrence	--	0.2	5.8	58.6	64.6	--	--	21.1	224.6	245.8
Lewis	--	1.2	7.6	53.6	62.5	--	2.0	26.6	192.5	221.1
Lincoln	--	0.9	14.3	125.6	140.7	--	--	51.3	459.3	510.6
Linn	--	--	9.6	25.1	34.7	--	--	22.9	70.4	93.3

(Table 59 continued on next page)

(Table 59 continued)

	Growing stock					Sawtimber				
	Major species group					Major species group				
	In million cubic feet					In million board feet [1]				
Forest Survey Unit and county	Pine	Other softwoods	Soft hardwoods	Hard hardwoods	All species	Pine	Other softwoods	Soft hardwoods	Hard hardwoods	All species
Prairie										
Livingston	--	2.1	18.7	22.6	43.5	--	6.4	69.8	79.4	155.5
Macon	--	0.2	36.7	58.6	95.5	--	--	133.5	142.2	275.7
Marion	--	0.0	18.3	53.8	72.1	--	--	59.6	196.9	256.5
Mercer	--	0.2	4.6	21.3	26.1	--	--	7.7	72.8	80.5
Monroe	--	1.0	20.4	83.6	104.9	--	--	56.2	247.9	304.1
Nodaway	--	--	0.7	10.7	11.4	--	--	--	38.6	38.6
Pettis	--	0.1	8.1	41.8	50.0	--	--	19.7	141.2	160.9
Pike	--	0.8	33.5	116.8	151.2	--	1.8	112.3	364.7	478.9
Platte	--	--	16.8	29.5	46.3	--	--	47.2	84.2	131.4
Putnam	--	--	6.3	39.6	45.9	--	--	16.1	155.7	171.7
Ralls	--	0.5	2.3	32.3	35.1	--	--	4.5	107.9	112.4
Randolph	--	--	9.8	64.2	73.9	--	--	35.3	232.0	267.3
Ray	--	0.3	25.4	18.1	43.8	--	--	86.8	58.4	145.3
Saline	--	0.2	27.6	69.9	97.7	--	--	104.7	253.1	357.8
Schuyler	--	--	0.0	33.7	33.7	--	--	--	80.5	80.5
Scotland	--	0.2	12.0	23.2	35.4	--	--	30.5	60.3	90.8
Shelby	--	--	7.4	40.6	48.0	--	--	25.3	137.5	162.8
Sullivan	--	0.3	24.9	74.3	99.5	--	--	93.6	261.3	354.9
Vernon	--	--	47.1	32.1	79.2	--	--	163.7	111.1	274.8
Worth	--	--	9.1	5.1	14.1	--	--	41.9	23.0	65.0
Total	0.3	20.9	773.8	2,118.5	2,913.5	1.7	33.7	2,524.3	7,107.0	9,666.7

(Table 59 continued on next page)

(Table 59 continued)

Forest Survey Unit and county	Growing stock					Sawtimber				
	Major species group					Major species group				
	In million cubic feet					In million board feet [1]				
	Pine	Other softwoods	Soft hardwoods	Hard hardwoods	All species	Pine	Other softwoods	Soft hardwoods	Hard hardwoods	All species
Riverborder										
Boone	--	12.6	26.0	134.6	173.2	--	37.1	83.7	442.7	563.4
Callaway	--	16.5	16.3	193.4	226.3	--	51.8	43.1	634.2	729.1
Cape Girardeau	1.3	--	23.0	106.9	131.1	4.6	--	83.4	416.9	504.8
Cole	--	15.2	5.8	73.4	94.4	--	50.0	11.2	232.6	293.7
Dunklin	--	--	3.3	4.0	7.3	--	--	11.0	17.8	28.7
Franklin	1.2	28.1	24.2	243.6	297.0	4.9	86.2	74.4	846.1	1,011.5
Gasconade	--	7.1	12.4	164.1	183.6	--	16.8	39.2	506.4	562.5
Howard	--	3.4	24.5	54.2	82.1	--	9.2	87.9	176.8	273.9
Jefferson	7.5	32.4	18.6	209.6	268.1	39.4	88.6	52.3	693.9	874.1
Mississippi	--	--	23.3	6.8	30.1	--	--	88.5	29.3	117.7
Moniteau	--	2.3	4.4	35.6	42.3	--	7.8	13.9	117.7	139.5
Montgomery	--	3.0	5.0	93.3	101.3	--	5.4	12.8	322.8	341.0
New Madrid	--	--	18.3	1.2	19.5	--	--	71.2	--	71.2
Osage	--	16.2	8.7	169.9	194.9	--	39.7	11.5	541.1	592.2
Perry	0.5	2.1	11.2	121.5	135.3	1.9	5.0	26.2	425.2	458.3
St. Charles	--	6.0	23.9	84.0	113.9	--	16.0	85.1	300.1	401.3
Ste. Genevieve	10.3	17.8	11.4	186.6	226.2	46.1	42.7	26.4	652.1	767.3
St. Louis	--	1.1	12.5	62.3	75.9	--	4.2	41.2	247.2	292.6
Scott	--	--	12.1	18.6	30.7	--	--	46.2	73.1	119.3
Stoddard	2.0	0.1	9.9	34.1	46.2	--	--	19.7	128.9	148.6
Warren	3.1	1.8	16.7	200.0	221.6	13.5	3.6	55.7	757.7	830.5
Total	25.9	165.8	311.3	2,197.8	2,700.8	110.4	464.1	984.4	7,562.4	9,121.3
All counties	754.8	427.4	1,541.6	11,633.1	14,357.0	3,122.3	943.8	4,728.7	36,784.9	45,579.8

All table cells without observations in the inventory sample are indicated by --. Table value of 0.0 indicates the volume rounds to less than 0.1 million cubic or board feet. Columns and rows may not add to their totals due to rounding.
[1] International 1/4-inch rule.

Table 59a -- Net volume of growing-stock and sawtimber (Doyle rule) on timberland by Forest Survey Unit, county, and major species group, Missouri, 1999-2003

Forest Survey Unit and county	Growing stock					Sawtimber				
	Major species group					Major species group				
	Pine	Other softwoods	Soft hardwoods	Hard hardwoods	All species	Pine	Other softwoods	Soft hardwoods	Hard hardwoods	All species
	In million cubic feet					In million board feet [1]				
Eastern Ozarks										
Butler	19.2	0.3	20.6	135.8	176.0	42.1	0.7	30.4	267.4	340.5
Carter	61.7	1.1	9.5	226.5	298.8	135.1	2.4	9.9	379.8	527.2
Crawford	1.3	5.8	24.7	277.2	309.0	1.4	6.5	44.8	472.5	525.2
Dent	28.9	1.9	4.0	252.2	287.1	64.5	1.0	4.4	390.5	460.4
Iron	19.0	2.8	7.4	253.8	283.0	39.0	2.3	7.2	407.5	456.0
Madison	28.1	4.5	10.6	215.9	259.1	58.1	3.6	11.8	398.6	472.2
Oregon	39.3	0.9	3.8	230.7	274.7	95.8	0.9	3.3	430.2	530.2
Reynolds	70.8	3.0	20.9	362.4	457.1	145.6	3.2	34.6	571.6	755.0
Ripley	45.2	2.0	21.9	210.5	279.6	133.7	1.6	27.5	316.5	479.1
St. Francois	11.2	8.7	10.0	123.7	153.6	15.2	7.7	16.5	216.9	256.3
Shannon	82.9	4.9	14.7	395.4	497.9	181.0	6.2	20.0	678.0	885.2
Washington	54.6	7.6	10.5	329.5	402.2	134.2	4.8	10.7	556.4	706.0
Wayne	66.3	2.0	23.5	355.7	447.5	157.1	2.0	29.5	600.3	788.9
Total	528.5	45.6	182.1	3,369.3	4,125.5	1,202.6	43.0	250.5	5,686.0	7,182.1
Southwestern Ozarks										
Barry	14.1	13.7	5.9	168.2	201.9	23.3	8.2	4.9	329.1	365.5
Christian	2.7	9.1	7.8	104.4	123.9	7.3	4.9	18.8	183.8	214.8
Douglas	19.6	4.9	7.2	187.9	219.7	62.0	2.5	11.6	297.1	373.2
Howell	37.8	0.3	3.3	262.9	304.2	85.1	- -	4.2	405.9	495.2
McDonald	3.5	3.2	8.2	170.8	185.7	12.1	5.3	3.3	321.7	342.4
Newton	- -	1.3	4.0	178.2	183.6	- -	2.5	- -	433.1	435.6
Ozark	18.8	12.5	15.0	180.8	227.1	50.4	6.2	22.0	303.7	382.2
Stone	- -	22.6	3.5	95.5	121.5	- -	20.2	3.5	139.2	162.9
Taney	5.2	39.3	6.5	153.6	204.6	3.9	35.0	4.7	253.2	296.7
Texas	82.2	3.9	10.7	302.6	399.4	161.1	1.5	2.7	443.8	609.1
Webster	- -	1.6	5.1	158.2	164.9	- -	- -	6.0	314.2	320.2
Wright	0.4	5.6	28.9	143.1	178.0	- -	2.6	66.5	239.8	308.9
Total	184.3	118.0	106.1	2,106.3	2,514.6	405.1	89.0	148.1	3,664.5	4,306.7

(Table 59a continued on next page)

93

	Growing stock					Sawtimber				
	Major species group					Major species group				
	In million cubic feet					In million board feet [1]				
Forest Survey Unit and county	Pine	Other softwoods	Soft hardwoods	Hard hardwoods	All species	Pine	Other softwoods	Soft hardwoods	Hard hardwoods	All species
Northwestern Ozarks										
Benton	--	10.4	9.3	216.3	236.0	--	9.2	15.3	365.7	390.2
Camden	--	2.1	1.9	203.1	207.1	--	--	2.6	381.6	384.2
Cedar	--	3.7	58.6	49.7	111.9	--	7.1	170.4	87.3	264.8
Dallas	--	9.0	10.2	130.3	149.5	--	10.4	14.8	209.7	235.0
Hickory	--	8.7	2.1	78.3	89.1	--	4.9	1.1	114.0	120.0
Laclede	7.5	5.6	9.3	201.5	223.9	10.3	4.3	15.8	361.7	392.0
Maries	--	13.6	4.2	123.8	141.5	--	9.9	4.0	201.6	215.5
Miller	--	4.0	8.6	152.3	164.9	--	2.5	14.0	264.2	280.7
Morgan	--	1.7	7.2	183.9	192.8	--	0.7	10.8	353.6	365.1
Phelps	7.2	7.3	3.7	155.7	173.9	18.7	5.7	3.9	204.6	232.9
Polk	--	4.7	10.1	71.9	86.7	--	2.0	14.3	110.5	126.8
Pulaski	1.2	4.0	32.3	156.5	194.0	2.5	2.8	83.0	241.6	329.9
St. Clair	--	2.4	10.8	118.0	131.1	--	1.9	18.0	208.9	228.7
Total	15.9	77.0	168.3	1,841.3	2,102.5	31.5	61.4	368.0	3,104.9	3,565.8

(Table 59a continued on next page)

94

(Table 59a continued)

Forest Survey Unit and county	Growing stock					Sawtimber				
	Major species group					Major species group				
	Pine	Other softwoods	Soft hardwoods	Hard hardwoods	All species	Pine	Other softwoods	Soft hardwoods	Hard hardwoods	All species
	In million cubic feet					In million board feet [1]				
Prairie										
Adair	- -	0.2	4.0	54.6	58.7	- -	- -	0.9	79.7	80.6
Andrew	- -	- -	27.5	5.6	33.1	- -	- -	118.7	15.8	134.5
Atchison	- -	- -	12.2	15.0	27.1	- -	- -	24.7	39.7	64.4
Audrain	- -	- -	23.1	61.0	84.2	- -	- -	55.1	112.3	167.4
Barton	- -	- -	11.0	40.7	51.8	- -	- -	14.2	91.9	106.1
Bates	- -	0.1	21.4	36.9	58.4	- -	- -	44.0	84.6	128.6
Buchanan	- -	- -	36.4	20.4	56.8	- -	- -	90.0	37.5	127.4
Caldwell	- -	- -	4.0	3.9	7.9	- -	- -	6.3	3.4	9.7
Carroll	- -	- -	0.5	2.8	3.3	- -	- -	- -	5.5	5.5
Cass	- -	0.6	26.6	60.9	88.1	- -	0.5	30.8	145.1	176.3
Chariton	- -	0.5	12.0	48.9	61.4	- -	0.6	15.6	85.2	101.4
Clark	- -	1.2	5.5	27.4	34.1	- -	1.0	3.6	54.2	58.8
Clay	0.3	- -	19.3	18.4	38.0	0.6	- -	58.3	56.1	115.0
Clinton	- -	- -	- -	1.1	1.1	- -	- -	- -	3.0	3.0
Cooper	- -	3.0	10.1	42.8	55.9	- -	0.9	33.2	98.0	132.1
Dade	- -	0.1	12.4	45.8	58.3	- -	- -	22.7	96.3	118.9
Daviess	- -	- -	9.5	55.3	64.9	- -	- -	21.6	112.3	133.9
DeKalb	- -	- -	6.8	7.3	14.2	- -	- -	9.0	16.5	25.5
Gentry	- -	- -	9.6	49.9	59.4	- -	- -	14.4	102.9	117.3
Greene	- -	1.9	13.8	85.5	101.2	- -	1.1	29.8	187.7	218.5
Grundy	- -	- -	10.6	14.7	25.3	- -	- -	26.5	16.5	43.0
Harrison	- -	0.1	12.7	51.6	64.4	- -	- -	19.3	105.7	125.1
Henry	- -	4.7	23.4	45.1	73.2	- -	7.5	59.2	81.5	148.2
Holt	- -	0.0	6.5	16.4	22.9	- -	- -	13.1	34.3	47.4
Jackson	- -	- -	51.5	41.1	92.6	- -	- -	179.5	104.2	283.7
Jasper	- -	- -	11.1	25.2	36.4	- -	- -	10.8	56.1	66.8
Johnson	- -	0.2	10.9	62.2	73.2	- -	- -	18.7	119.4	138.1
Knox	- -	0.1	8.9	29.1	38.1	- -	- -	14.5	58.2	72.8
Lafayette	- -	- -	5.5	14.3	19.8	- -	- -	4.7	32.4	37.1
Lawrence	- -	0.2	5.8	58.6	64.6	- -	- -	15.6	138.9	154.5
Lewis	- -	1.2	7.6	53.6	62.5	- -	0.9	13.2	110.4	124.6
Lincoln	- -	0.9	14.3	125.6	140.7	- -	- -	33.6	265.6	299.3
Linn	- -	- -	9.6	25.1	34.7	- -	- -	15.7	51.9	67.6

(Table 59a continued on next page)

	Growing stock					Sawtimber				
	Major species group					Major species group				
Forest Survey Unit and county	Pine	Other softwoods	Soft hardwoods	Hard hardwoods	All species	Pine	Other softwoods	Soft hardwoods	Hard hardwoods	All species
	In million cubic feet					In million board feet[1]				
Prairie										
Livingston	--	2.1	18.7	22.6	43.5	--	2.2	44.8	52.0	99.1
Macon	--	0.2	36.7	58.6	95.5	--	--	94.0	77.6	171.6
Marion	--	0.0	18.3	53.8	72.1	--	--	37.7	147.1	184.8
Mercer	--	0.2	4.6	21.3	26.1	--	--	4.1	37.4	41.5
Monroe	--	1.0	20.4	83.6	104.9	--	--	32.9	173.6	206.5
Nodaway	--	--	0.7	10.7	11.4	--	--	--	20.7	20.7
Pettis	--	0.1	8.1	41.8	50.0	--	--	10.9	88.9	99.7
Pike	--	0.8	33.5	116.8	151.2	--	0.6	102.8	210.0	313.5
Platte	--	--	16.8	29.5	46.3	--	--	28.5	64.7	93.2
Putnam	--	--	6.3	39.6	45.9	--	--	8.6	97.0	105.7
Ralls	--	0.5	2.3	32.3	35.1	--	--	1.9	62.8	64.7
Randolph	--	--	9.8	64.2	73.9	--	--	22.7	130.9	153.6
Ray	--	0.3	25.4	18.1	43.8	--	--	63.6	29.1	92.7
Saline	--	0.2	27.6	69.9	97.7	--	--	80.9	155.8	236.7
Schuyler	--	--	0.0	33.7	33.7	--	--	--	45.1	45.1
Scotland	--	0.2	12.0	23.2	35.4	--	--	17.8	46.2	64.0
Shelby	--	--	7.4	40.6	48.0	--	--	13.9	86.1	100.0
Sullivan	--	0.3	24.9	74.3	99.5	--	--	84.3	160.8	245.1
Vernon	--	--	47.1	32.1	79.2	--	--	95.0	65.3	160.3
Worth	--	--	9.1	5.1	14.1	--	--	30.2	13.7	43.9
Total	0.3	20.9	773.8	2,118.5	2,913.5	0.6	15.2	1,791.9	4,367.5	6,175.2

(Table 59a continued on next page)

(Table 59a continued)

	Growing stock					Sawtimber				
	Major species group					Major species group				
	In million cubic feet					In million board feet[1]				
Forest Survey Unit and county	Pine	Other softwoods	Soft hardwoods	Hard hardwoods	All species	Pine	Other softwoods	Soft hardwoods	Hard hardwoods	All species
Riverborder										
Boone	--	12.6	26.0	134.6	173.2	--	18.5	59.1	267.8	345.4
Callaway	--	16.5	16.3	193.4	226.3	--	26.4	23.1	373.0	422.5
Cape Girardeau	1.3	--	23.0	106.9	131.1	2.0	--	50.0	252.2	304.2
Cole	--	15.2	5.8	73.4	94.4	--	23.0	5.8	147.7	176.6
Dunklin	--	--	3.3	4.0	7.3	--	--	5.9	9.2	15.1
Franklin	1.2	28.1	24.2	243.6	297.0	2.7	45.3	56.0	494.4	598.4
Gasconade	--	7.1	12.4	164.1	183.6	--	7.9	27.2	295.7	330.8
Howard	--	3.4	24.5	54.2	82.1	--	4.3	70.0	98.3	172.6
Jefferson	7.5	32.4	18.6	209.6	268.1	26.7	42.4	30.5	419.0	518.6
Mississippi	--	--	23.3	6.8	30.1	--	--	63.2	20.0	83.2
Moniteau	--	2.3	4.4	35.6	42.3	--	3.5	7.5	67.3	78.3
Montgomery	--	3.0	5.0	93.3	101.3	--	2.2	7.0	192.3	201.6
New Madrid	--	--	18.3	1.2	19.5	--	--	47.0	--	47.0
Osage	--	16.2	8.7	169.9	194.9	--	19.0	6.1	313.2	338.3
Perry	0.5	2.1	11.2	121.5	135.3	0.7	1.7	15.4	252.7	270.5
St. Charles	--	6.0	23.9	84.0	113.9	--	7.6	53.7	205.0	266.3
Ste. Genevieve	10.3	17.8	11.4	186.6	226.2	25.1	19.0	15.5	394.9	454.4
St. Louis	--	1.1	12.5	62.3	75.9	--	1.8	28.9	173.5	204.1
Scott	--	--	12.1	18.6	30.7	--	--	28.2	50.8	79.0
Stoddard	2.0	0.1	9.9	34.1	46.2	--	--	10.9	90.8	101.6
Warren	3.1	1.8	16.7	200.0	221.6	7.2	2.0	53.2	447.2	509.6
Total	25.9	165.8	311.3	2,197.8	2,700.8	64.4	224.7	664.0	4,565.0	5,518.0
All counties	754.8	427.4	1,541.6	11,633.1	14,357.0	1,704.2	433.2	3,222.5	21,388.0	26,747.9

All table cells without observations in the inventory sample are indicated by --. Table value of 0.0 indicates the volume rounds to less than 0.1 million cubic or board feet. Columns and rows may not add to their totals due to rounding.
[1] Doyle rule.

Table 60. -- Average annual net growth of growing-stock and sawtimber (International 1/4-inch rule) on timberland by Forest Survey Unit, county, and major species group, Missouri, 1989 to 1999-2003

Forest Survey Unit and county	Growing stock Major species group (In million cubic feet)					Sawtimber Major species group (In million board feet)[1]				
	Pine	Other softwoods	Soft hardwoods	Hard hardwoods	All species	Pine	Other softwoods	Soft hardwoods	Hard hardwoods	All species
Eastern Ozarks										
Butler	1.2	- -	0.7	5.5	7.4	7.4	- -	0.5	24.3	32.2
Carter	2.7	0.0	0.9	8.9	12.4	13.1	- -	1.3	35.9	50.2
Crawford	- -	0.6	1.4	10.4	12.3	- -	1.3	3.5	47.0	51.8
Dent	1.1	0.0	0.5	12.6	14.2	6.8	- -	1.8	41.9	50.5
Iron	0.3	0.0	0.3	7.5	8.1	2.6	- -	0.4	34.3	37.4
Madison	0.2	0.3	0.5	7.6	8.6	0.9	0.7	1.8	31.8	35.3
Oregon	0.7	0.1	0.1	8.3	9.2	4.2	- -	0.7	42.0	46.9
Reynolds	0.9	0.1	0.1	11.4	12.4	4.6	0.2	0.8	40.6	46.2
Ripley	0.9	0.1	1.8	9.7	12.5	4.7	0.8	5.4	40.7	51.5
St. Francois	- -	1.7	0.6	4.1	6.5	- -	3.5	2.7	15.8	21.9
Shannon	1.0	0.0	0.5	16.3	17.9	5.1	- -	1.7	75.0	81.7
Washington	0.8	0.2	0.6	10.0	11.5	4.6	0.1	1.2	45.0	50.9
Wayne	1.1	-0.1	1.5	9.4	12.0	5.2	-0.3	4.9	35.1	44.8
Total	10.9	2.8	9.7	121.7	145.0	59.2	6.3	26.6	509.3	601.4
Southwestern Ozarks										
Barry	0.2	0.9	0.3	6.7	8.1	0.9	0.8	1.3	25.7	28.7
Christian	- -	0.3	0.3	4.0	4.5	- -	0.5	1.2	12.3	14.1
Douglas	0.7	0.2	0.1	8.1	9.1	3.4	0.2	0.0	32.7	36.3
Howell	1.0	0.1	0.3	11.9	13.3	6.2	0.7	1.3	38.3	46.6
McDonald	- -	0.1	0.2	10.7	11.0	- -	0.9	-0.6	44.9	45.3
Newton	- -	0.1	0.4	5.8	6.3	- -	- -	- -	24.9	24.9
Ozark	0.2	0.4	0.8	7.6	9.1	2.1	0.2	0.6	25.6	28.4
Stone	- -	1.6	- -	4.7	6.3	- -	5.3	- -	15.9	21.1
Taney	0.2	2.9	0.8	8.9	12.8	0.7	5.8	1.3	28.2	35.9
Texas	3.2	0.5	0.6	11.9	16.1	13.6	0.8	0.8	43.5	58.8
Webster	- -	- -	0.1	6.2	6.3	- -	- -	0.8	24.6	25.3
Wright	0.1	0.3	0.4	6.7	7.4	1.1	0.6	1.0	21.4	24.2
Total	5.5	7.3	4.3	93.0	110.2	28.1	15.7	7.8	337.9	389.5

(Table 60 continued on next page)

(Table 60 continued)

Forest Survey Unit and county	Growing stock					Sawtimber				
	Major species group					Major species group				
	(In million cubic feet)					(In million board feet)[1]				
	Pine	Other softwoods	Soft hardwoods	Hard hardwoods	All species	Pine	Other softwoods	Soft hardwoods	Hard hardwoods	All species
Northwestern Ozarks										
Benton	--	0.4	0.5	12.7	13.6	--	0.4	1.5	38.9	40.8
Camden	--	0.2	0.1	8.9	9.3	--	--	0.6	31.2	31.8
Cedar	--	0.2	3.3	2.3	5.8	--	1.0	12.6	9.6	23.3
Dallas	--	0.5	0.5	5.1	6.1	--	0.1	1.8	20.1	22.0
Hickory	--	0.5	-0.1	2.9	3.3	--	1.6	--	7.1	8.7
Laclede	1.5	0.4	0.6	10.9	13.4	8.8	0.7	1.7	37.2	48.4
Maries	--	0.8	0.0	6.7	7.5	--	1.2	-0.4	20.6	21.4
Miller	--	0.5	0.5	5.6	6.6	--	0.4	1.7	18.0	20.1
Morgan	--	0.4	0.3	7.9	8.6	--	0.5	1.0	29.9	31.4
Phelps	0.3	0.1	0.0	7.8	8.3	1.5	0.4	0.4	28.9	31.2
Polk	--	0.7	1.1	3.5	5.3	--	2.2	0.5	12.0	14.7
Pulaski	--	0.2	0.7	7.0	8.0	--	1.3	-0.1	21.6	22.7
St. Clair	--	0.3	0.8	10.1	11.2	--	1.2	1.4	29.0	31.7
Total	1.8	5.2	8.4	91.3	106.8	10.3	11.2	22.5	304.2	348.2

(Table 60 continued on next page)

99

(Table 60 continued)

	Growing stock Major species group (In million cubic feet)					Sawtimber Major species group (In million board feet) [1]				
Forest Survey Unit and county	Pine	Other softwoods	Soft hardwoods	Hard hardwoods	All species	Pine	Other softwoods	Soft hardwoods	Hard hardwoods	All species
Prairie										
Adair	--	0.0	0.3	2.4	2.7	--	--	1.1	7.5	8.6
Audrain	--	--	1.6	3.2	4.7	--	--	5.3	14.2	19.5
Barton	--	--	0.8	1.4	2.2	--	--	3.7	5.4	9.1
Bates	--	--	1.1	1.8	2.9	--	--	3.6	8.2	11.7
Buchanan	--	--	0.3	1.3	1.6	--	--	0.9	4.0	4.9
Caldwell	--	--	0.3	0.3	0.6	--	--	1.1	0.5	1.6
Carroll	--	--	--	0.2	0.2	--	--	--	1.1	1.1
Cass	--	0.1	2.4	3.9	6.3	--	0.2	5.0	12.5	17.7
Chariton	--	--	1.3	1.8	3.1	--	--	1.3	7.3	8.6
Clark	--	-0.1	0.2	2.2	2.4	--	--	0.2	8.4	8.6
Clay	--	--	1.1	0.9	2.0	--	--	3.9	3.8	7.7
Cooper	--	0.1	0.9	4.6	5.6	--	--	4.0	13.7	17.8
Dade	--	0.0	2.6	3.2	5.8	--	--	9.3	13.2	22.5
Daviess	--	--	0.2	2.7	2.9	--	--	1.2	7.5	8.7
DeKa b	--	--	--	0.0	0.0	--	--	--	--	--
Gentry	--	--	0.8	3.3	4.0	--	--	2.7	12.3	15.1
Greene	--	0.3	1.1	4.1	5.5	--	0.1	1.7	16.0	17.7
Grundy	--	--	0.6	1.1	1.7	--	--	2.9	4.5	7.4
Harrison	--	0.1	1.1	2.4	3.6	--	--	2.8	9.3	12.1
Henry	--	0.4	1.0	2.3	3.6	--	1.8	3.7	5.4	10.8
Holt	--	--	0.1	0.2	0.3	--	--	0.6	1.2	1.8
Jackson	--	--	1.7	2.1	3.9	--	--	4.8	5.7	10.5
Jasper	--	--	0.6	1.2	1.9	--	--	1.0	3.3	4.3
Johnson	--	--	0.3	3.4	3.7	--	--	0.7	14.8	15.5
Knox	--	0.0	0.7	1.5	2.2	--	--	2.4	6.9	9.3
Lafayette	--	--	0.7	0.7	1.4	--	--	1.2	3.2	4.4
Lawrence	--	0.0	0.5	1.6	2.1	--	--	2.3	6.9	9.3
Lewis	--	-0.1	0.4	1.4	1.7	--	-0.3	1.3	8.3	9.3
Lincoln	--	0.2	0.5	3.3	4.0	--	--	1.1	13.5	14.7
Linn	--	--	0.0	2.0	2.0	--	--	0.0	3.1	3.1
Livingston	--	0.2	2.1	1.8	4.1	--	--	0.9	9.1	6.3	16.2
Macon	--	--	-0.4	2.0	1.6	--	--	-4.7	6.2	1.5
Marion	--	--	0.3	3.5	3.8	--	--	1.4	13.7	15.1

(Table 60 continued on next page)

100

(Table 60 continued)

Forest Survey Unit and county	Growing stock					Sawtimber				
	Major species group					Major species group				
			(In million cubic feet)					(In million board feet)[1]		
	Pine	Other softwoods	Soft hardwoods	Hard hardwoods	All species	Pine	Other softwoods	Soft hardwoods	Hard hardwoods	All species
Prairie										
Mercer	--	--	0.3	0.7	1.0	--	--	1.6	2.3	3.9
Monroe	--	0.0	2.3	3.5	5.8	--	--	3.9	11.0	14.9
Nodaway	--	--	--	0.4	0.4	--	--	--	1.2	1.2
Pettis	--	--	0.3	2.3	2.5	--	--	0.7	8.8	9.5
Pike	--	--	0.4	5.6	6.0	--	--	4.3	18.1	22.4
Platte	--	--	-0.1	1.6	1.5	--	--	--	7.1	7.1
Putnam	--	--	0.6	1.1	1.7	--	--	0.6	4.8	5.4
Ralls	--	--	0.1	2.1	2.3	--	--	0.1	8.1	8.3
Randolph	--	--	0.0	2.5	2.5	--	--	0.5	10.1	10.6
Ray	--	--	0.3	0.5	0.8	--	--	0.4	1.1	1.5
Saline	--	--	0.8	2.0	2.8	--	--	2.0	7.2	9.1
Schuyler	--	--	0.0	2.0	1.9	--	--	-0.1	3.8	3.8
Scotland	--	--	0.4	2.6	3.0	--	--	1.2	9.6	10.8
Shelby	--	--	0.4	1.5	2.0	--	--	1.5	6.3	7.8
Sullivan	--	--	1.5	1.8	3.3	--	--	6.4	6.6	13.0
Vernon	--	--	2.2	2.4	4.6	--	--	9.6	5.3	14.9
Total	--	1.5	34.8	100.1	136.3	--	2.5	108.2	359.3	470.0

(Table 60 continued on next page)

101

(Table 60 continued)

Forest Survey Unit and county	Growing stock (In million cubic feet)					Sawtimber (In million board feet)[1]				
	Major species group				All species	Major species group				All species
	Pine	Other softwoods	Soft hardwoods	Hard hardwoods		Pine	Other softwoods	Soft hardwoods	Hard hardwoods	
Riverborder										
Boone	--	2.0	0.7	11.8	14.5	--	6.2	1.5	41.0	48.7
Callaway	--	0.6	1.5	8.6	10.7	--	1.3	4.8	28.6	34.7
Cape Girardeau	--	--	1.4	5.8	7.2	--	--	4.3	28.0	32.4
Cole	--	1.5	0.3	6.3	8.1	--	6.3	0.5	20.9	27.7
Dunklin	--	--	0.0	0.0	0.1	--	--	0.1	0.1	0.3
Franklin	--	0.4	0.3	11.3	12.0	--	1.9	0.7	42.9	45.5
Gasconade	--	0.5	1.5	8.7	10.7	--	2.5	7.8	27.2	37.4
Howard	--	--	2.8	2.4	5.2	--	--	11.7	12.4	24.0
Jefferson	0.1	1.2	0.3	11.5	13.0	0.4	2.7	1.1	43.4	47.6
Moniteau	--	0.3	0.1	1.3	1.7	--	1.0	--	5.3	6.4
Montgomery	--	0.1	0.6	2.6	3.3	--	0.2	0.8	9.1	10.0
Osage	--	0.8	0.7	8.3	9.8	--	4.5	2.1	34.7	41.2
Pemiscot	--	--	0.4	0.0	0.4	--	--	1.6	0.1	1.7
Perry	--	--	0.2	2.6	2.8	--	--	-0.1	13.4	13.3
St. Charles	--	0.3	0.6	3.6	4.5	--	1.1	3.3	17.4	21.8
Ste. Genevieve	0.1	0.6	0.2	7.0	7.8	0.2	1.0	-0.3	33.7	34.6
St. Louis	--	--	0.9	3.1	4.1	--	--	2.9	11.2	14.1
Scott	--	--	0.2	0.9	1.1	--	--	0.8	4.3	5.1
Stoddard	--	0.0	0.4	0.1	0.5	--	0.1	--	-1.2	-1.1
Warren	0.5	-0.3	1.8	6.4	8.4	3.0	-0.4	4.4	32.5	39.5
Total	0.6	8.2	14.9	102.1	125.9	3.6	28.3	47.9	405.0	484.8
All counties	18.8	25.1	72.1	508.2	624.2	101.3	64.0	213.0	1,915.7	2,294.0

All table cells without observations in the inventory sample are indicated by --. Table value of 0.0 indicates the volume rounds to less than 0.1 million cubic or board feet. Columns and rows may not add to their totals due to rounding.
[1] International 1/4-inch rule.

Table 60a — Average annual net growth of growing-stock and sawtimber (Doyle rule) on timberland by Forest Survey Unit, county, and major species group, Missouri, 1989 to 1999-2003

Forest Survey Unit and county	Growing stock (In million cubic feet)					Sawtimber (In million board feet)[1]				
	Major species group					Major species group				
	Pine	Other softwoods	Soft hardwoods	Hard hardwoods	All species	Pine	Other softwoods	Soft hardwoods	Hard hardwoods	All species
Eastern Ozarks										
Butler	1.2	--	0.7	5.5	7.4	3.6	--	0.3	13.6	17.4
Carter	2.7	0.0	0.9	8.9	12.4	6.1	--	0.7	19.4	26.2
Crawford	--	0.6	1.4	10.4	12.3	--	0.5	1.7	24.9	27.1
Dent	1.1	0.0	0.5	12.6	14.2	3.1	--	1.0	22.5	26.7
Iron	0.3	0.0	0.3	7.5	8.1	1.3	--	0.3	16.7	18.4
Madison	0.2	0.3	0.5	7.6	8.6	0.6	0.3	0.8	17.0	18.6
Oregon	0.7	0.1	0.1	8.3	9.2	2.4	--	0.4	21.3	24.0
Reynolds	0.9	0.1	0.1	11.4	12.4	2.4	0.2	0.1	19.6	22.2
Ripley	0.9	0.1	1.8	9.7	12.5	3.1	0.3	2.6	19.6	25.6
St. Francois	--	1.7	0.6	4.1	6.5	--	1.5	1.4	9.2	12.1
Shannon	1.0	0.0	0.5	16.3	17.9	3.0	--	1.1	40.8	44.8
Washington	0.8	0.2	0.6	10.0	11.5	2.5	0.0	0.6	22.5	25.6
Wayne	1.1	-0.1	1.5	9.4	12.0	2.6	-0.1	2.2	17.1	21.8
Total	10.9	2.8	9.7	121.7	145.0	30.8	2.6	13.0	264.2	310.6
Southwestern Ozarks										
Barry	0.2	0.9	0.3	6.7	8.1	0.7	0.4	0.6	13.6	15.3
Christian	--	0.3	0.3	4.0	4.5	--	0.2	1.0	6.8	8.0
Douglas	0.7	0.2	0.1	8.1	9.1	2.0	0.1	0.0	16.5	18.7
Howell	1.0	0.1	0.3	11.9	13.3	2.1	0.3	0.6	19.0	22.1
McDonald	--	0.1	0.2	10.7	11.0	--	0.3	-0.4	25.5	25.4
Newton	--	0.1	0.4	5.8	6.3	--	--	--	14.4	14.4
Ozark	0.2	0.4	0.8	7.6	9.1	0.8	0.1	0.4	13.0	14.3
Stone	--	1.6	--	4.7	6.3	--	2.0	--	8.5	10.5
Taney	0.2	2.9	0.8	8.9	12.8	0.3	2.4	0.8	16.3	19.8
Texas	3.2	0.5	0.6	11.9	16.1	6.9	0.3	0.6	23.1	30.9
Webster	--	--	0.1	6.2	6.3	--	--	0.3	14.1	14.4
Wright	0.1	0.3	0.4	6.7	7.4	0.4	0.3	0.5	10.6	11.8
Total	5.5	7.3	4.3	93.0	110.2	13.2	6.5	4.3	181.4	205.4

(Table 60a continued on next page)

103

Forest Survey Unit and county	Growing stock Major species group (In million cubic feet)					Sawtimber Major species group (In million board feet) [1]				
	Pine	Other softwoods	Soft hardwoods	Hard hardwoods	All species	Pine	Other softwoods	Soft hardwoods	Hard hardwoods	All species
Northwestern Ozarks										
Benton	--	0.4	0.5	12.7	13.6	--	0.1	0.6	21.4	22.2
Camden	--	0.2	0.1	8.9	9.3	--	--	0.4	17.0	17.5
Cedar	--	0.2	3.3	2.3	5.8	--	0.6	9.0	6.9	16.5
Dallas	--	0.5	0.5	5.1	6.1	--	0.1	0.9	13.1	14.0
Hickory	--	0.5	-0.1	2.9	3.3	--	0.5	--	3.6	4.2
Laclede	1.5	0.4	0.6	10.9	13.4	3.6	0.3	1.3	21.1	26.3
Maries	--	0.8	0.0	6.7	7.5	--	0.4	-0.3	13.4	13.5
Miller	--	0.5	0.5	5.6	6.6	--	0.2	1.9	10.2	12.3
Morgan	--	0.4	0.3	7.9	8.6	--	0.2	0.7	17.3	18.2
Phelps	0.3	0.1	0.0	7.8	8.3	1.0	0.2	0.2	15.2	16.6
Polk	--	0.7	1.1	3.5	5.3	--	0.8	0.2	6.4	7.4
Pulaski	--	0.2	0.7	7.0	8.0	--	0.4	-0.1	12.0	12.4
St. Clair	--	0.3	0.8	10.1	11.2	--	0.6	1.3	17.0	18.9
Total	1.8	5.2	8.4	91.3	106.8	4.7	4.4	16.1	174.8	200.0

(Table 60a continued on next page)

104

Prairie

Forest Survey Unit and county	Growing stock					Sawtimber				
	Major species group (In million cubic feet)					Major species group (In million board feet) [1]				
	Pine	Other softwoods	Soft hardwoods	Hard hardwoods	All species	Pine	Other softwoods	Soft hardwoods	Hard hardwoods	All species
Adair	--	0.0	0.3	2.4	2.7	--	--	0.5	3.8	4.3
Audrain	--	--	1.6	3.2	4.7	--	--	4.1	9.4	13.5
Barton	--	--	0.8	1.4	2.2	--	--	1.8	3.1	4.9
Bates	--	--	1.1	1.8	2.9	--	--	2.2	3.5	5.7
Buchanan	--	--	0.3	1.3	1.6	--	--	0.6	2.8	3.5
Caldwell	--	--	0.3	0.3	0.6	--	--	0.7	0.3	1.0
Carroll	--	--	--	0.2	0.2	--	--	--	0.7	0.7
Cass	--	0.1	2.4	3.9	6.3	--	0.1	4.5	8.0	12.6
Chariton	--	--	1.3	1.8	3.1	--	--	0.9	4.0	4.9
Clark	--	-0.1	0.2	2.2	2.4	--	--	0.1	5.1	5.2
Clay	--	--	1.1	0.9	2.0	--	--	3.6	2.5	6.1
Cooper	--	0.1	0.9	4.6	5.6	--	--	2.3	8.1	10.4
Dade	--	0.0	2.6	3.2	5.8	--	--	6.2	9.2	15.4
Daviess	--	--	0.2	2.7	2.9	--	--	0.8	4.2	4.9
DeKalb b	--	--	--	0.0	0.0	--	--	--	--	--
Gentry	--	--	0.8	3.3	4.0	--	--	1.7	8.2	9.9
Greene	--	0.3	1.1	4.1	5.5	--	0.0	1.0	9.7	10.7
Grundy	--	--	0.6	1.1	1.7	--	--	1.6	2.1	3.7
Harrison	--	0.1	1.1	2.4	3.6	--	--	1.5	5.4	6.9
Henry	--	0.4	1.0	2.3	3.6	--	1.1	2.3	3.2	6.6
Holt	--	--	0.1	0.2	0.3	--	--	0.5	0.7	1.2
Jackson	--	--	1.7	2.1	3.9	--	--	3.7	4.5	8.2
Jasper	--	--	0.6	1.2	1.9	--	--	0.6	1.7	2.4
Johnson	--	--	0.3	3.4	3.7	--	--	0.4	8.9	9.3
Knox	--	0.0	0.7	1.5	2.2	--	--	1.3	4.3	5.6
Lafayette	--	--	0.7	0.7	1.4	--	--	0.7	2.3	3.1
Lawrence	--	0.0	0.5	1.6	2.1	--	--	1.7	4.0	5.7
Lewis	--	-0.1	0.4	1.4	1.7	--	-0.2	0.8	4.5	5.1
Lincoln	--	0.2	0.5	3.3	4.0	--	--	0.5	7.5	8.0
Linn	--	--	0.0	2.0	2.0	--	--	0.0	1.8	1.8
Livingston	--	0.2	2.1	1.8	4.1	--	0.3	5.9	2.8	9.0
Macon	--	--	-0.4	2.0	1.6	--	--	-3.9	3.1	-0.9
Marion	--	--	0.3	3.5	3.8	--	--	0.9	8.8	9.7

(Table 60a continued on next page)

	Growing stock					Sawtimber				
	Major species group					Major species group				
Forest Survey Unit and county	Pine	Other softwoods	Soft hardwoods	Hard hardwoods	All species	Pine	Other softwoods	Soft hardwoods	Hard hardwoods	All species
	(In million cubic feet)					(In million board feet) [1]				
Prairie										
Mercer	- -	- -	0.3	0.7	1.0	- -	- -	0.9	1.0	1.8
Monroe	- -	0.0	2.3	3.5	5.8	- -	- -	2.3	5.5	7.8
Nodaway	- -	- -	- -	0.4	0.4	- -	- -	- -	0.6	0.6
Pettis	- -	- -	0.3	2.3	2.5	- -	- -	0.3	4.8	5.1
P ke	- -	- -	0.4	5.6	6.0	- -	- -	2.0	9.9	11.9
Platte	- -	- -	-0.1	1.6	1.5	- -	- -	- -	4.0	4.0
Putnam	- -	- -	0.6	1.1	1.7	- -	- -	0.3	2.9	3.2
Ralls	- -	- -	0.1	2.1	2.3	- -	- -	0.0	4.4	4.4
Randolph	- -	- -	0.0	2.5	2.5	- -	- -	0.2	5.8	6.0
Ray	- -	- -	0.3	0.5	0.8	- -	- -	0.2	0.5	0.7
Saline	- -	- -	0.8	2.0	2.8	- -	- -	1.2	4.2	5.5
Schuyler	- -	- -	0.0	2.0	1.9	- -	- -	0.0	1.9	1.9
Scotland	- -	- -	0.4	2.6	3.0	- -	- -	1.5	8.0	9.5
Shelby	- -	- -	0.4	1.5	2.0	- -	- -	0.7	4.2	4.8
Sullivan	- -	- -	1.5	1.8	3.3	- -	- -	4.9	4.0	8.9
Vernon	- -	- -	2.2	2.4	4.6	- -	- -	6.0	2.9	8.9
Total	- -	1.5	34.8	100.1	136.3	- -	1.3	70.0	212.7	284.0

(Table 60a continued on next page)

106

(Table 60a continued)

Forest Survey Unit and county	Growing stock					Sawtimber				
	Major species group					Major species group				
	Pine	Other softwoods	Soft hardwoods	Hard hardwoods	All species	Pine	Other softwoods	Soft hardwoods	Hard hardwoods	All species
	(In million cubic feet)					(In million board feet) [1]				
Riverborder										
Boone	--	2.0	0.7	11.8	14.5	--	2.6	0.8	24.2	27.6
Callaway	--	0.6	1.5	8.6	10.7	--	0.1	2.8	15.8	18.7
Cape Girardeau	--	--	1.4	5.8	7.2	--	--	2.3	13.8	16.1
Cole	--	1.5	0.3	6.3	8.1	--	2.7	0.2	11.4	14.3
Dunklin	--	--	0.0	0.0	0.1	--	--	0.1	0.1	0.2
Franklin	--	0.4	0.3	11.3	12.0	--	0.9	0.5	24.6	26.0
Gasconade	--	0.5	1.5	8.7	10.7	--	0.9	3.1	14.7	18.6
Howard	--	--	2.8	2.4	5.2	--	--	10.7	6.8	17.6
Jefferson	0.1	1.2	0.3	11.5	13.0	0.3	0.9	0.6	24.8	26.6
Moniteau	--	0.3	0.1	1.3	1.7	--	0.6	--	3.1	3.7
Montgomery	--	0.1	0.6	2.6	3.3	--	0.1	0.4	4.9	5.4
Osage	--	0.8	0.7	8.3	9.8	--	1.5	1.0	20.6	23.0
Pemiscot	--	--	0.4	0.0	0.4	--	--	0.8	0.1	0.9
Perry	--	--	0.2	2.6	2.8	--	--	0.0	7.1	7.1
St. Charles	--	0.3	0.6	3.6	4.5	--	0.5	2.8	10.2	13.6
Ste. Genevieve	0.1	0.6	0.2	7.0	7.8	0.1	0.4	-0.1	19.1	19.5
St. Louis	--	--	0.9	3.1	4.1	--	--	1.8	7.0	8.8
Scott	--	--	0.2	0.9	1.1	--	--	0.6	3.5	4.1
Stoddard	--	0.0	0.4	0.1	0.5	--	0.1	--	-1.2	-1.1
Warren	0.5	-0.3	1.8	6.4	8.4	1.8	-0.2	4.0	18.0	23.7
Total	0.6	8.2	14.9	102.1	125.9	2.2	11.1	32.3	228.8	274.4
All counties	18.8	25.1	72.1	508.2	624.2	50.9	26.0	135.6	1,061.8	1,274.3

All table cells without observations in the inventory sample are indicated by --. Table value of 0.0 indicates the volume rounds to less than 0.1 million cubic or board feet. Columns and rows may not add to their totals due to rounding.
[1] Doyle rule.

107

Table 61. -- Average annual removals of growing-stock and sawtimber (International 1/4-inch rule) on timberland by Forest Survey Unit, county, and major species group. Missouri, 1989 to 1999-2003

| Forest Survey Unit and county | Growing stock (In million cubic feet) | | | | | Sawtimber (In million board feet)[1] | | | | |
| | Major species group | | | | | Major species group | | | | |
	Pine	Other softwoods	Soft hardwoods	Hard hardwoods	All species	Pine	Other softwoods	Soft hardwoods	Hard hardwoods	All species
Eastern Ozarks										
Butler	1.1	- -	0.2	1.7	2.9	5.6	- -	0.8	6.9	13.2
Carter	0.2	- -	- -	1.7	1.9	1.0	- -	- -	7.3	8.4
Crawford	- -	0.0	0.3	1.3	1.7	- -	- -	1.5	4.4	6.0
Dent	0.1	- -	0.1	0.9	1.2	0.7	- -	- -	2.1	2.8
Iron	0.6	- -	- -	1.3	2.0	3.2	- -	- -	4.7	7.9
Madison	0.3	- -	- -	4.0	4.2	1.5	- -	- -	12.0	13.5
Oregon	0.6	- -	0.3	3.6	4.5	3.4	- -	0.7	14.3	18.3
Reynolds	0.7	- -	- -	4.5	5.1	3.3	- -	- -	15.6	18.9
Ripley	0.1	- -	- -	4.5	4.6	0.7	- -	- -	21.6	22.3
St. Francois	- -	0.1	0.5	1.1	1.6	- -	- -	1.5	4.4	5.9
Shannon	0.2	- -	- -	4.4	4.6	1.1	- -	- -	19.6	20.7
Washington	0.5	- -	- -	3.6	4.0	2.5	- -	- -	12.4	14.8
Wayne	0.1	0.1	0.4	4.8	5.3	0.4	- -	1.8	19.8	22.1
Total	4.5	0.2	1.7	37.2	43.6	23.5	- -	6.4	145.0	174.8
Southwestern Ozarks										
Barry	- -	0.2	- -	0.7	0.9	- -	0.5	- -	3.5	4.0
Christian	- -	- -	- -	0.3	0.3	- -	- -	- -	0.6	0.6
Douglas	0.1	- -	- -	2.2	2.3	0.6	- -	- -	8.8	9.4
Howell	1.9	- -	- -	3.4	5.3	8.0	- -	- -	9.9	17.9
McDonald	- -	- -	- -	1.9	1.9	- -	- -	- -	4.3	4.3
Newton	- -	- -	- -	0.7	0.7	- -	- -	- -	2.5	2.5
Ozark	0.1	- -	0.1	2.5	2.6	0.4	- -	- -	7.7	8.1
Stone	- -	0.1	- -	0.1	0.2	- -	- -	- -	- -	- -
Taney	- -	0.3	- -	0.1	0.4	- -	1.0	- -	- -	1.0
Texas	2.0	- -	0.3	3.1	5.4	7.4	- -	1.3	11.2	19.9
Webster	- -	- -	- -	3.0	3.0	- -	- -	- -	13.7	13.7
Wright	- -	- -	- -	1.2	1.2	- -	- -	- -	5.1	5.1
Total	4.0	0.6	0.4	19.1	24.1	16.5	1.5	1.3	67.2	86.6

(Table 61 continued on next page)

(Table 61 continued)

Forest Survey Unit and county	Growing stock					Sawtimber				
	Major species group (In million cubic feet)					Major species group (In million board feet)[1]				
	Pine	Other softwoods	Soft hardwoods	Hard hardwoods	All species	Pine	Other softwoods	Soft hardwoods	Hard hardwoods	All species
Northwestern Ozarks										
Benton	--	0.2	0.1	0.9	1.2	--	0.6	0.5	3.3	4.4
Camden	--	--	--	0.2	0.2	--	--	--	1.0	1.0
Cedar	--	--	--	0.5	0.5	--	--	--	2.0	2.0
Dallas	--	--	--	0.2	0.2	--	--	--	1.1	1.1
Hickory	--	--	--	0.1	0.1	--	--	--	--	--
Laclede	--	--	--	1.2	1.2	--	--	--	3.8	3.8
Maries	--	--	--	0.2	0.2	--	--	--	0.9	0.9
Miller	--	--	--	1.8	1.8	--	--	--	8.0	8.0
Morgan	--	--	--	1.2	1.2	--	--	--	2.1	2.1
Phelps	--	0.1	--	2.2	2.2	--	--	--	8.3	8.3
Polk	--	0.3	--	0.6	0.9	--	--	--	2.8	2.8
Pulaski	--	0.1	0.1	1.3	1.5	--	--	--	4.1	4.1
St. Clair	--	--	0.1	0.4	0.5	--	--	--	1.0	1.0
Total	--	0.7	0.3	10.8	11.7	--	0.6	0.5	38.4	39.5

(Table 61 continued on next page)

109

(Table 61 continued)

Forest Survey Unit and county	Growing stock — Major species group (In million cubic feet)					Sawtimber — Major species group (In million board feet) [1]				
	Pine	Other softwoods	Soft hardwoods	Hard hardwoods	All species	Pine	Other softwoods	Soft hardwoods	Hard hardwoods	All species
Prairie										
Barton	--	--	0.8	0.7	1.5	--	--	3.8	2.0	5.8
Bates	--	--	--	0.9	0.9	--	--	--	3.9	3.9
Buchanan	--	--	--	0.2	0.2	--	--	--	0.8	0.8
Chariton	--	--	1.7	0.1	1.8	--	--	7.2	0.7	7.9
Dade	--	--	0.1	0.1	0.2	--	--	--	--	--
Gentry	--	--	--	0.3	0.3	--	--	--	--	--
Greene	--	0.2	0.1	0.4	0.6	--	0.5	--	1.7	2.2
Harrison	--	--	0.4	0.3	0.7	--	--	1.9	0.6	2.5
Henry	--	--	--	0.2	0.2	--	--	--	1.2	1.2
Jasper	--	--	--	0.3	0.3	--	--	--	1.4	1.4
Knox	--	--	0.1	0.5	0.6	--	--	0.4	2.4	2.8
Lafayette	--	--	0.9	--	0.9	--	--	4.0	--	4.0
Lincoln	--	--	--	2.1	2.1	--	--	--	9.9	9.9
Linn	--	--	0.1	--	0.1	--	--	0.5	--	0.5
Macon	--	--	0.3	0.1	0.4	--	--	1.3	0.6	2.0
Monroe	--	--	--	0.7	0.7	--	--	--	2.9	2.9
Nodaway	--	--	--	0.1	0.1	--	--	--	0.5	0.5
Pike	--	--	0.6	0.2	0.9	--	--	3.1	1.0	4.1
Putnam	--	--	0.1	--	0.1	--	--	--	--	--
Ralls	--	--	--	1.7	1.7	--	--	--	7.8	7.8
Randolph	--	--	--	0.1	0.1	--	--	--	0.7	0.7
Saline	--	--	--	0.2	0.2	--	--	--	1.1	1.1
Schuyler	--	--	0.2	--	0.2	--	--	0.5	--	0.5
Scotland	--	--	0.1	0.6	0.7	--	--	0.6	2.6	3.2
Vernon	--	--	0.1	0.2	0.4	--	--	0.6	1.1	1.7
Total	--	0.2	5.7	10.1	15.9	--	0.5	23.8	43.0	67.3

(Table 61 continued on next page)

110

(Table 61 continued)

Forest Survey Unit and county	Growing stock					Sawtimber				
	Major species group (In million cubic feet)					Major species group (In million board feet) [1]				
	Pine	Other softwoods	Soft hardwoods	Hard hardwoods	All species	Pine	Other softwoods	Soft hardwoods	Hard hardwoods	All species
Riverborder										
Boone	--	--	--	0.1	0.1	--	--	--	--	--
Callaway	--	0.1	0.3	1.8	2.2	--	0.6	1.3	6.7	8.6
Cape Girardeau	--	--	--	0.9	0.9	--	--	--	4.5	4.5
Cole	--	--	--	1.3	1.3	--	--	--	4.5	4.5
Dunklin	--	--	0.2	0.3	0.5	--	--	0.5	1.2	1.7
Franklin	--	0.1	--	1.2	1.3	--	--	--	2.5	2.5
Gasconade	--	--	--	0.6	0.6	--	--	--	1.8	1.8
Howard	--	--	--	0.6	0.6	--	--	--	2.7	2.7
Jefferson	--	0.4	--	1.0	1.4	--	0.9	--	3.8	4.7
Moniteau	--	--	--	0.4	0.4	--	--	--	0.8	0.8
Osage	--	0.3	--	0.9	1.2	--	1.1	--	4.0	5.0
Pemiscot	--	--	1.3	0.2	1.5	--	--	5.3	0.8	6.1
St. Charles	--	--	1.2	1.5	2.6	--	--	5.4	3.8	9.2
Ste. Genevieve	--	0.1	--	1.2	1.3	--	--	--	3.8	3.8
St. Louis	--	--	--	0.3	0.3	--	--	--	1.3	1.3
Scott	--	--	0.4	0.8	1.2	--	--	2.1	4.1	6.2
Stoddard	--	0.4	--	0.8	1.3	--	2.0	--	1.7	3.8
Warren	--	--	--	2.0	2.0	--	--	--	8.4	8.4
Total	--	1.4	3.4	16.0	20.7	--	4.6	14.6	56.4	75.5
All counties	8.6	3.0	11.3	93.2	116.1	40.0	7.2	46.6	350.0	443.7

All table cells without observations in the inventory sample are indicated by --. Table value of 0.0 indicates the volume rounds to less than 0.1 million cubic or board feet. Columns and rows may not add to their totals due to rounding.
[1] International 1/4-inch rule.

Table 61a. — Average annual removals of growing stock and sawtimber (Doyle rule) on timberland by Forest Survey Unit, county, and major species group, Missouri, 1989 to 1999-2003

	Growing stock					Sawtimber				
	Major species group					Major species group				
	(In million cubic feet)					(In million board feet) [1]				
Forest Survey Unit and county	Pine	Other softwoods	Soft hardwoods	Hard hardwoods	All species	Pine	Other softwoods	Soft hardwoods	Hard hardwoods	All species
Eastern Ozarks										
Butler	1.1	--	0.2	1.7	2.9	3.1	--	0.4	2.8	6.3
Carter	0.2	--	--	1.7	1.9	0.2	--	--	4.1	4.3
Crawford	--	0.0	0.3	1.3	1.7	--	--	0.9	2.2	3.1
Dent	0.1	--	0.1	0.9	1.2	0.2	--	--	0.9	1.1
Iron	0.6	--	--	1.3	2.0	1.5	--	--	2.0	3.5
Madison	0.3	--	--	4.0	4.2	0.8	--	--	5.3	6.1
Oregon	0.6	--	0.3	3.6	4.5	2.1	--	0.4	7.2	9.7
Reynolds	0.7	--	--	4.5	5.1	1.5	--	--	5.5	7.0
Ripley	0.1	--	--	4.5	4.6	0.4	--	--	11.2	11.6
St. Francois	--	0.1	0.5	1.1	1.6	--	--	0.8	2.9	3.7
Shannon	0.2	--	--	4.4	4.6	0.5	--	--	9.8	10.3
Washington	0.5	--	--	3.6	4.0	1.2	--	--	6.3	7.5
Wayne	0.1	0.1	0.4	4.8	5.3	0.2	--	1.1	9.6	10.9
Total	4.5	0.2	1.7	37.2	43.6	11.8	--	3.5	69.8	85.2
Southwestern Ozarks										
Barry	--	0.2	--	0.7	0.9	--	0.2	--	1.7	1.9
Christian	--	--	--	0.3	0.3	--	--	--	0.4	0.4
Douglas	0.1	--	--	2.2	2.3	0.3	--	--	4.8	5.1
Howell	1.9	--	--	3.4	5.3	3.1	--	--	4.7	7.8
McDonald	--	--	--	1.9	1.9	--	--	--	1.5	1.5
Newton	--	--	--	0.7	0.7	--	--	--	1.6	1.6
Ozark	0.1	--	0.1	2.5	2.6	0.2	--	--	4.7	5.0
Stone	--	0.1	--	0.1	0.2	--	--	--	--	--
Taney	--	0.3	--	0.1	0.4	--	0.4	--	--	0.4
Texas	2.0	--	0.3	3.1	5.4	4.2	--	0.7	5.3	10.2
Webster	--	--	--	3.0	3.0	--	--	--	8.5	8.5
Wright	--	--	--	1.2	1.2	--	--	--	2.2	2.2
Total	4.0	0.6	0.4	19.1	24.1	7.8	0.5	0.7	35.4	44.4

(Table 61a continued on next page)

112

(Table 61a continued)

Forest Survey Unit and county	Growing stock (In million cubic feet)					Sawtimber (In million board feet)[1]				
	Major species group					Major species group				
	Pine	Other softwoods	Soft hardwoods	Hard hardwoods	All species	Pine	Other softwoods	Soft hardwoods	Hard hardwoods	All species
Northwestern Ozarks										
Benton	--	0.2	0.1	0.9	1.2	--	0.2	0.2	1.9	2.4
Camden	--	--	--	0.2	0.2	--	--	--	0.5	0.5
Cedar	--	--	--	0.5	0.5	--	--	--	1.2	1.2
Dallas	--	--	--	0.2	0.2	--	--	--	0.7	0.7
Hickory	--	--	--	0.1	0.1	--	--	--	--	--
Laclede	--	--	--	1.2	1.2	--	--	--	1.8	1.8
Maries	--	--	--	0.2	0.2	--	--	--	0.5	0.5
Miller	--	--	--	1.8	1.8	--	--	--	4.9	4.9
Morgan	--	--	--	1.2	1.2	--	--	--	0.9	0.9
Phelps	--	0.1	--	2.2	2.2	--	--	--	4.4	4.4
Polk	--	0.3	--	0.6	0.9	--	--	--	1.4	1.4
Pulaski	--	0.1	0.1	1.3	1.5	--	--	--	1.8	1.8
St. Clair	--	--	0.1	0.4	0.5	--	--	--	0.4	0.4
Total	--	0.7	0.3	10.8	11.7	--	0.2	0.2	20.5	21.0

(Table 61a continued on next page)

113

Forest Survey Unit and county	Growing stock Major species group (In million cubic feet)					Sawtimber Major species group (In million board feet)[1]				
	Pine	Other softwoods	Soft hardwoods	Hard hardwoods	All species	Pine	Other softwoods	Soft hardwoods	Hard hardwoods	All species
Prairie										
Barton	--	--	0.8	0.7	1.5	--	--	2.4	1.3	3.8
Bates	--	--	--	0.9	0.9	--	--	--	0.8	0.8
Buchanan	--	--	--	0.2	0.2	--	--	--	0.7	0.7
Chariton	--	--	1.7	0.1	1.8	--	--	6.5	0.5	7.0
Dade	--	--	0.1	0.1	0.2	--	--	--	--	--
Gentry	--	--	--	0.3	0.3	--	--	--	--	--
Greene	--	0.2	0.1	0.4	0.6	--	0.2	--	0.9	1.0
Harrison	--	--	0.4	0.3	0.7	--	--	0.8	0.3	1.2
Henry	--	--	--	0.2	0.2	--	--	--	0.6	0.6
Jasper	--	--	--	0.3	0.3	--	--	--	0.7	0.7
Knox	--	--	0.1	0.5	0.6	--	--	0.2	2.1	2.2
Lafayette	--	--	0.9	--	0.9	--	--	4.0	--	4.0
Lincoln	--	--	--	2.1	2.1	--	--	--	5.5	5.5
Linn	--	--	0.1	0.1	0.1	--	--	0.3	--	0.3
Macon	--	--	0.3	0.1	0.4	--	--	0.8	0.4	1.2
Monroe	--	--	--	0.7	0.7	--	--	--	2.2	2.2
Nodaway	--	--	--	0.1	0.1	--	--	--	0.4	0.4
P ke	--	--	0.6	0.2	0.9	--	--	2.1	0.7	2.8
Putnam	--	--	0.1	--	0.1	--	--	--	--	--
Ralls	--	--	--	1.7	1.7	--	--	--	4.4	4.4
Randolph	--	--	--	0.1	0.1	--	--	--	0.5	0.5
Saline	--	--	--	0.2	0.2	--	--	--	0.8	0.8
Schuyler	--	--	0.2	--	0.2	--	--	0.3	--	0.3
Scotland	--	--	0.1	0.6	0.7	--	--	0.4	2.0	2.4
Vernon	--	--	0.1	0.2	0.4	--	--	0.4	0.9	1.3
Total	--	0.2	5.7	10.1	15.9	--	0.2	18.2	25.7	44.0

(Table 61a continued on next page)

114

(Table 61a continued)

| Forest Survey Unit and county | Growing stock | | | | | Sawtimber | | | | |
| | Major species group (In million cubic feet) | | | | | Major species group (In million board feet)[1] | | | | |
	Pine	Other softwoods	Soft hardwoods	Hard hardwoods	All species	Pine	Other softwoods	Soft hardwoods	Hard hardwoods	All species
Riverborder										
Boone	--	--	--	0.1	0.1	--	--	--	--	--
Callaway	--	0.1	0.3	1.8	2.2	--	--	0.7	3.8	4.5
Cape Girardeau	--	--	--	0.9	0.9	--	--	--	3.0	3.0
Cole	--	--	--	1.3	1.3	--	--	--	2.5	2.5
Dunklin	--	--	0.2	0.3	0.5	--	--	0.2	1.1	1.4
Franklin	--	0.1	--	1.2	1.3	--	--	--	1.4	1.4
Gasconade	--	--	--	0.6	0.6	--	--	--	1.1	1.1
Howard	--	--	--	0.6	0.6	--	--	--	1.8	1.8
Jefferson	--	0.4	--	1.0	1.4	--	0.4	--	2.0	2.4
Moniteau	--	--	--	0.4	0.4	--	--	--	0.5	0.5
Osage	--	0.3	--	0.9	1.2	--	0.2	--	2.1	2.3
Pemiscot	--	--	1.3	0.2	1.5	--	--	3.0	0.6	3.5
St. Charles	--	--	1.2	1.5	2.6	--	--	4.0	2.2	6.3
Ste. Genevieve	--	0.1	--	1.2	1.3	--	--	--	2.1	2.1
St. Louis	--	--	--	0.3	0.3	--	--	--	0.6	0.6
Scott	--	--	0.4	0.8	1.2	--	--	1.1	2.6	3.6
Stoddard	--	0.4	--	0.8	1.3	--	1.9	--	1.2	3.1
Warren	--	--	--	2.0	2.0	--	--	--	4.9	4.9
Total	--	1.4	3.4	16.0	20.7	--	2.5	9.0	33.5	45.0
All counties	8.6	3.0	11.3	93.2	116.1	19.6	3.4	31.7	184.8	239.5

All table cells without observations in the inventory sample are indicated by -- . Table value of 0.0 indicates the volume rounds to less than 0.1 million cubic or board feet. Columns and rows may not add to their totals due to rounding.
[1] Doyle rule.

115